Documents and Debates
General Editor: John Wroughton M.A., F.R.Hist.S.

1.95

D0601351

Sixteenth-Century Europe

Katherine Leach

History Mistress, The Royal School, Bath

Macmillan Education

First published 1980

Published by
MACMILLAN EDUCATION LIMITED
Houndmills Basingstoke Hampshire RG21 2XS
and London
Associated companies in Delhi   Dublin
Hong Kong   Johannesburg   Lagos   Melbourne
New York   Singapore and Tokyo

Printed in Hong Kong

British Library Cataloguing in Publication Data

Leach, Katherine
Sixteenth century Europe. – (Documents and debates).
1. Europe – History – 1492–1648
I. Title   II. Series
940.2'32   D228

ISBN 0–333–27500–4

Contents

General Editor's Preface

This book forms part of a series entitled *Documents and Debates*, which is aimed primarily at the sixth form. Each volume covers approximately one century of either English or European history and consists of ten or eleven sections, each dealing with a major theme. In most cases a varied selection of documents will bring evidence to bear on the chosen theme, supplemented by a stimulating extract from a modern historian. A few 'Debate' sections, however, will centre on the most important controversies of each century. Here extracts from the changing opinions of modern research, normally found only in learned journals and expensive monographs, will be made available in manageable form. The series intends partly to provide experience for those pupils who are required to answer questions on documentary extracts at 'A' Level, and partly to provide pupils of all abilities with a digestible and interesting collection of source material, which will extend the normal textbook approach.

This book is designed essentially for the pupil's own personal use. The author's introduction will put the century as a whole into perspective, highlighting the central issues, main controversies, available source material and recent developments. Although it is clearly not our intention to replace the traditional textbook, each section will carry its own brief introduction, which will set the documents into context. The short, select bibliography is intended to encourage the pupil to follow up issues raised in the section by further reading – without being subjected to the off-putting experience of an exhaustive list. A wide variety of source material has been used in order to give the pupils the maximum amount of experience – letters, speeches, newspapers, memoirs, diaries, official papers, Acts of Parliament, Minute Books, accounts, local documents, family papers, etc. The questions vary in difficulty, but aim throughout to compel the pupil to think in depth by the use of unfamiliar material. Historical knowledge and understanding will be tested, as well as basic comprehension. Pupils will also be encouraged by the questions to assess the reliability of evidence, to recognise bias and emotional prejudice, to reconcile conflicting accounts and to extract the essential from the irrelevant. Some questions, marked with an asterisk, require knowledge outside the immediate extract and are intended for further research or discussion, based on the pupil's general knowledge of the period. Finally, we hope that students using this material will learn something of the nature of historical inquiry and the role of the historian.

John Wroughton

Acknowledgements

The author and publishers wish to thank the following who have kindly given permission for the use of copyright material:

George Allen & Unwin (Publishers) Ltd for extracts from *Government & Society in France* by J. H. Shennan; Edward Arnold (Publishers) Ltd for extracts from *Erasmus: Documents in Modern History* by DeMolen, *Huldrych Zwingli* by Potter, and *Luther* by Rupp & Drewery from the series *Documents in Modern History*; Associated Book Publishers Ltd for an extract from *Aspects of European History 1494–1789* by Stephen J. Lee published by Methuen & Co. Ltd; Ernest Benn Ltd for an extract from *The Revolt in the Netherlands* by Pieter Geyl (Second Edition, Fifth Impression 1980); Adam and Charles Black (Publishers) Ltd for an extract from *The European Dynamic* by Margaret Shennan; Bobbs-Merrill Educational Publishing for extracts from *Constitutionalism and Resistance in the 16th Century* by J. M. Franklin; Cambridge University Press for extracts from *The Old World and the New* by J. H. Elliott, and *Texts Concerning the Revolt of the Netherlands* edited by E. H. Kossmann and A. F. Mellink; Jonathan Cape Ltd on behalf of the Executors of the Karl Brandi Estate for an extract from *The Emperor Charles V* translated by C. V. Wedgewood, and on behalf of the Executors of the Garrett Mattingly Estate for an extract from *The Defeat of the Spanish Armada*; Wm Collins Sons & Co. Ltd for extracts from *The Mediterranean and the Mediterranean World in the Age of Philip II* Vol. II by Fernand Braudel; Constable & Company Ltd for an extract from *The Spanish Terror* by Maurice Rowdon; Glencoe Publishing Co. Inc. for an extract from *The Catholic Reformation*, Revised Edition by Pierre Janelle © 1949, 1963 The Bruce Publishing Company; Granada Publishing Ltd Paul Elek Ltd for an extract from *The Discovery of South America* by J. H. Parry; A. M. Heath on behalf of Ernle Bradford for extracts from *The Sultan's Admiral* and *The Great Siege of Malta*; The Historical Association for an extract from *Francis I and Absolute Monarchy* by R. J. Knecht; Hutchinson Publishing Group Limited for extracts from *Europe and a Wider World 1415–1715* by J. H. Parry, and *Origins of the Modern European State* by J. H. Sharman; Macmillan Publishing Co. Inc. for extracts from *Renaissance and Reformation 1300–1648* by G. R. Elton; John Murray (Publishers) Ltd for an extract from *Europe 1450–1815* by E. J. Knapton; Oxford University Press for an extract from *Early Modern France 1560–1717* by Robin Briggs; The Past and Present Society for extracts from articles published in *Past and Present*, a journal of historical studies, by Geoffrey Parker (November 1970, February 1973), Andrew C. Hess (November 1972) and Henry Kamen (November 1978); Penguin Books Ltd for extracts from Baldesar Castiglione *The Book of the Courtier*, translated by George Bull, Machiavelli *The Prince* translated by George Bull, and Machiavelli *The Discourses* translated by Leslie J. Walker edited by Bernard Crick; Prentice-Hall Inc., Englewood Cliffs, New Jersey, for an extract from *The Age of Humanism and Reformation* by A. G. Dickens; Sage Publications Ltd for an extract from the article 'Counter-Reformation Cardinals' by A. V. Antonovics in *European Studies Review* Vol. 2 No. 4, 1972; Thames and Hudson Ltd for extracts from *Parliament and Estates in Europe to 1789*, by A. R. Myers, and *The Ottoman Impact on Europe* by Paul Coles; University of California Press for an extract from *The Christian Century in Japan 1549–1650* by C. R. Boxer; Weidenfeld & Nicholson Ltd for extracts from *The Spanish Inquisition* (1965) by H. Kamen, and an extract from *St. Bartholomew's Night* by P. Erlanger; Charles Wilson for extracts from his *Queen Elizabeth and the Revolt of the Netherlands*.

The author and publishers also thank the Bibliothèque Publique et Universitaire de Genève for their kind permission in allowing us to reproduce the cover illustration.

Europe in the
Sixteenth Century

In the middle of the nineteenth century Thomas Carlyle wrote about 'the three great elements of modern civilization, Gunpowder, Printing and the Protestant Religion'. The sixteenth century has traditionally been regarded as the beginning of the modern world and the reason why it was so different from the essentially medieval fifteenth century was the development of Carlyle's 'elements of modern civilization' and certain other changes, though all of them had actually begun in the fifteenth century.

Probably the most important of these changes were the invention of printing, about 1450, and the opening up of the world by the voyages of discovery. Printing made possible the rapid spread of ideas and information, among an increasingly literate society. The voyages of discovery widened men's horizons, mentally as well as physically, and although it was some time before the idea of a new world across the Atlantic was generally accepted, it did eventually become an ordinary part of men's knowledge of the world in which they lived. The other effects of the discovery included the availability of a greater variety of foodstuffs and a vast new source of silver. There had been a shortage of precious metals in Europe for many years, despite increased production from the silver mines of the Holy Roman Empire and the gold which reached Portugal from West Africa. The opening up of the mines at Potosí in Peru suddenly provided a great increase in Europe's supply of silver and this was one reason for the serious inflation from which Europe suffered during the second half of the sixteenth century. Of course this was not the only cause of inflation, but was part of a much more complex picture. Other factors were the considerable growth in Europe's population during the century, possibly as much as twenty-five per cent, more trade with the countries of the Far East, whose goods had largely to be paid for by exports of gold and silver, and the greatly increased cost and duration of wars, which were a very heavy drain on governments' revenues. Philip II of Spain's bankruptcies were the most serious and spectacular manifestations of a ruler's financial difficulties during the century, but his problems were shared to some extent by all contemporary princes.

The other great change which separated the sixteenth century from the Middle Ages was the break-up of Christendom. The idea of 'Europe' as an entity in its own right had only developed during the fifteenth century. Even Europe, however, was still generally seen as being united by the fact that all accepted the pope as head of the church, however many doubts and reservations there might be at different times. The advent of Luther in 1517 changed that. For the first time men had a choice of what to believe, a choice which was further enlarged when the ideas of Zwingli, Calvin, the Anabaptists and others became known. It is difficult for those who live in the twentieth century to realise what problems this posed, at least to educated men and women. Instead of a single church with clearly defined beliefs, which everyone was expected to accept, many people had, for the first time, to make a choice among two or more sets of doctrines, knowing that the 'wrong' choice might lead even to the stake. It is to the credit of many men and women that they were prepared to face these dangers for the sake of their faith, although there were probably far more who just accepted, with more or less willingness, whatever changes in doctrine and practice their rulers chose to introduce.

At the beginning of the century it had been obvious that the church needed reforming and so, in some ways, the Reformation was inevitable. What was perhaps not inevitable was the permanent division of Christendom into Roman Catholic and protestant churches, but at least this division helped to ensure both that the reform was a thorough-going one and that the churches set themselves and their members higher and more truly Christian standards – though to people today their in-tolerance towards believers of other sects may seem very unchristian.

The first half of the sixteenth century was thus dominated·by Luther, but also by Charles v. This was not due to Charles' personality or actual achievements, but to the fact that he ruled such a large part of Europe. He had inherited land from each of his four grandparents and it was a considerable feat to hold it all together, though he himself must have realised that these vast dominions were really too much for one man, when he made the unprecedented decision to abdicate and to divide his lands between his son and his brother.

His reign was a period of constant war, mainly against the Turks and France. The former threatened Spain's trade in the Mediterranean and the Habsburg family lands in Austria. Under the sultan Suleiman the Magnificent, it proved possible for the Turks to conquer Hungary quite easily and Turkish pirates and the sultan's fleet controlled much of the Mediterranean. Charles had only one major victory, at Tunis in 1535, but he suffered no serious defeat. Against France things were more difficult. Francis I was the most absolute ruler in Europe and he was determined to conquer Milan and perhaps other land in Italy. Even the destruction of the French army at Pavia in 1525 and Francis' own capture and imprison-ment did not deter him and so long as he refused to accept defeat it was impossible for Charles to make a permanent peace.

There is a very clear dividing line in the political history of Europe at about 1559. Charles v's abdication and death more or less coincided with the signing of the treaty of Cateau-Cambrésis, which ended his wars against France, the death of Henry II of France and the accession of a weak, young king there and of Queen Elizabeth I in England. There was also a minor on the Portuguese throne, a female regent, Margaret of Parma, in the Netherlands and an emperor, Ferdinand I, who was more concerned to conquer Hungary than to take an active part in western European affairs. As a result the new king, Philip II, of Spain was the only adult male ruler in the area and this made him seem at least as dominant as his father had been, even though he had not inherited all of Charles' lands.

The pattern in the second half of the sixteenth century was quite different. Civil war in France and a revolt in the Netherlands not only severely weakened those countries but also provided plenty of opportunities for outside interference, which was one of the characteristics of this period. The Netherlanders themselves sought help at different times from France, the archduke Matthias and England, but ultimately achieved independence for the northern provinces largely through their own efforts. As in the Netherlands, a large part of the trouble in France was caused by religion – the struggle of the Huguenots to achieve at least a degree of toleration for themselves and the refusal of the ultra-catholic party to allow this, which eventually found expression in the formation of the Holy League. Just as France herself had intervened in the Netherlands, almost sending an army in 1572 and actually sending one, albeit unofficially, in 1578, when the duke of Anjou was briefly accepted as a possible ruler, so Spain in turn interfered in French affairs. This seemed essential to Philip II because he did not want to see a protestant ruling the country and so he was prepared to support a rival catholic claimant, and his apparent failure was in some senses a success because the protestant king, Henry IV, realised the need to change his religion to make his rule acceptable to the French people.

Philip II, despite his financial difficulties, also managed to retain control of all his lands, except for part of the Netherlands, and he added to them Portugal and its empire. In addition, his fleets defeated the Turks at the battle of Lepanto. Although this resounding victory was not effectively followed up, it helped to make possible a truce between Spain and the Ottoman empire and so enabled Philip to turn his attention to affairs elsewhere. Whether Spain suffered a serious decline during Philip's reign and that of his son is a subject of controversy, though it seems clear both that Spain was not nearly so strong economically as she appeared to contemporaries and that Philip's taxation and other policies helped to weaken her even further, so that she ceased to be a major European power during the seventeenth century.

Europe in 1600 was thus very different from what it had been in 1500. The main political changes were due to the religious split, which meant that all international problems acquired a religious dimension. However, the Edict of Nantes, issued by Henry IV in 1598, can be seen as a fitting end to the century. It concluded thirty-five years of civil war by stating that both catholicism and protestantism were to be legal in France, and so foreshadowed the solution later to be reached in the rest of Europe.

I Humanism

Introduction

Humanism may be described as the intellectual side of the Renaissance. It began with interest in classical literature, which led to a concern for contemporary history and politics. At the same time other scholars published biblical texts in the original languages and the writings of the early Christian fathers. The invention of printing about 1450 made it possible for books to be widely disseminated and for writers such as Erasmus to become famous throughout Europe. The international character of universities facilitated the spread of the New Learning in England, the Netherlands, Spain and Germany.

The very diversity of interests and writings in the early sixteenth century means that there is no overall theme in this section. Castiglione's *The Book of the Courtier* is a series of imaginary conversations supposed to have taken place at the court of the Duke of Urbino in 1506. In contrast, Machiavelli's *The Prince* is concerned with the specific situation in Florence after 1512; *The Discourses* is a more general work. These two books appear to offer very different prescriptions for government, but in both Machiavelli is concerned with the establishment of a system which will survive the vicissitudes of events rather than the construction of a theoretically ideal one.

Erasmus wrote on a great variety of topics, but he was particularly famous for his edition of the New Testament in Greek and for his attacks on the abuses of the pre-reformation church. Consequently it is not surprising that he should need to defend himself against charges of Lutheranism. Lefèvre d'Étaples was also, and almost exclusively, concerned with the improvement of the church, while Michel de Montaigne retired from public life in 1571 to devote himself to literature. The essay 'On Cannibals' was written after he had met some Brazilian Indians, but other essays cover a great range of subjects.

Further Reading

B. Castiglione, *The Book of the Courtier* (Penguin, 1967)

Erasmus, *Praise of Folly* (Penguin, 1971)

Myron P. Gilmore, *The World of Humanism 1453–1517* (Harper & Row, 1952)

J. R. Hale, *Machiavelli and Renaissance Italy* (English Universities Press, 1961)

N. Machiavelli, *The Prince* (Penguin, 1961)

(Ed.) James Bruce Ross and Mary Martin McLaughlin, *The Portable Renaissance Reader* (Penguin, 1977)

1 Humanism

The word humanism . . . implies a creative study of Greek and Roman civilization. The humanists desired to know the Ancient World as it had really existed, to divest it of the veils swathed about its forms by the Christian centuries, to understand its higher values for their own sake. At
5 first with mediocre success, they tried to emulate its creations. Some of them believed that through apprenticeship they or their successors might come to surpass the ancients and so add a new glory to the history of man. . . .

Without renouncing Christianity, the thinkers of the humanist
10 mainstream saw man as a comprehensible being standing midway between God and the lower orders of nature. . . . They saw darkness being dispelled and the way back to the Ancient World likely to prove also — at least for a future generation — the way forward into a glorious future. In practice they concerned themselves with a philosophy of
15 man. . . . While they drew methods and examples from ancient writers, they strove to think in a manner relative to the needs and welfare of modern man. . . . Again, while they hoped to attain new approaches to Christianity, the humanists enormously increased the secular content of thought and literature. Once for all, learning had emerged from the
20 cloister and the academic lectureroom to rejoin the human mainstream.

A. G. Dickens, *The Age of Humanism and Reformation*, 1977, pp 4–6

Questions

a Why is 'humanism' an appropriate name?

b In what ways did the humanists try to emulate the Ancient World and in what ways did they break away from it?

* *c* How did this concern for the Ancient World help to cause the Reformation?

d In what sense did learning emerge 'from the cloister and the academic lectureroom' (lines 19–20)?

* *e* What recent development enabled the writings of the humanists to spread relatively easily and what was the significance of this for the future?

2 The Ideal Courtier

I would have our courtier of noble birth and good family, since it matters far less to a common man if he fails to perform virtuously and well than to a nobleman. . . .

I judge that the first and true profession of the courtier must be that of arms. . . . Let him also stand out from the rest as enterprising, bold and loyal to whomever he serves. And he will win a good reputation by demonstrating these qualities whenever and wherever possible. . . .

I wish our courtier to be well built, with finely proportioned members, and I would have him demonstrate strength and lightness and suppleness and be good at all the physical exercises befitting a warrior. . . .

The courtier should understand about seeking restitution and the conduct of disputes . . . and in all this he must show both courage and prudence. . . .

There are many other sports which, although they do not directly require the use of weapons, are closely related to arms. . . . Among these it seems to me that hunting is the most important, since in many ways it resembles warfare. . . .

It is enough if [the courtier] is, as we say, a man of honour and integrity. For this includes prudence, goodness, fortitude and temperance of soul, and all the other qualities proper to so honourable a man. . . .

I should like our courtier to be a more than average scholar, at least in those studies which we call the humanities; and he should have a knowledge of Greek as well as Latin. . . . He should be very well acquainted with the poets, and no less with the orators and historians, and also skilled at writing both verse and prose, especially in our own language; for in addition to the satisfaction this will give him personally, it will enable him to provide constant entertainment for the ladies. . . .

I must tell you that I am not satisfied with our courtier unless he is also a musician and unless as well as understanding and being able to read music he can play several instruments.

Baldesar Castiglione, *The Book of the Courtier*, 1528, trans. George Bull, 1967, pp 54, 57, 61–3, 87–90, 94

Questions

a   Why must 'the first and true profession of the courtier' (lines 4– 5) be that of arms?

*   b   Suggest examples of the 'poets . . . orators and historians' with whose works 'he should be very well acquainted' (lines 23 – 4).

*   c   Which of the attributes of a courtier, mentioned in the extract, had only come to be regarded as important during the Renaissance?

d   In your own words, describe the character of the courtier pictured by Castiglione. What other qualities do you think he would need?

3   How Princes Should Honour Their Word

Everyone realises how praiseworthy it is for a prince to honour his word

and to be straightforward rather than crafty in his dealings; nonetheless contemporary experience shows that princes who have achieved great things have been those who have given their word lightly, who have
5 known how to trick men with their cunning, and who, in the end, have overcome those abiding by honest principles. . . .

So it follows that a prudent ruler cannot, and should not, honour his word when it places him at a disadvantage and when the reasons for which he made his promise no longer exist. . . .
10 A prince, therefore, need not necessarily have all the good qualities I mentioned above, but he should certainly appear to have them. I would even go so far as to say that if he has these qualities and always behaves accordingly he will find them ruinous; if he only appears to have them they will render him service. He should appear to be compassionate,
15 faithful to his word, guileless and devout. And indeed he should be so. But his disposition should be such that, if he needs to be the opposite, he knows how. You must realise this: that a prince, and especially a new prince, cannot observe all those things which give men a reputation for virtue, because in order to maintain his state he is often forced to act in
20 defiance of good faith, of charity, of kindness, of religion. And so he should have a flexible disposition, varying as fortune and circumstances dictate. As I said above, he should not deviate from what is good, if that is possible, but he should know how to do evil, if that is necessary.

Niccolò Machiavelli, *The Prince*, 1513−14, trans. George Bull, 1961, pp 99−101

Questions

a   What qualities does Machiavelli believe a prince should appear to have and which should he actually have?

b   Why is it particularly important for 'a new prince' (lines 17−18) to gain a reputation for virtue?

*   c   Machiavelli claimed that he was writing on a basis of historical reality, not abstract ideals. From this extract, would you agree with him or do you think he was merely being cynical?

*   d   Why are Catherine de Medici and others so often accused of being 'Machiavellian'?

4   Various Forms of Government

Those who have written about states say that there are to be found in them one of the three forms of government, called by them *Principality*, *Aristocracy* and *Democracy*, and that those who set up a government in any particular state must adopt one of them, as best suits their purpose.
5 Others − and with better judgement many think − say that there are six types of government, of which three are very bad, and three are good in themselves but easily become corrupt, so that they too must be classed

as pernicious. Those that are good are the three above mentioned. Those
that are bad are the other three, which depend on them, and each of them
10 is so like the one associated with it that it easily passes from one form to
the other. For *Principality* easily becomes *Tyranny*. From *Aristocracy* the
transition to *Oligarchy* is an easy one. *Democracy* is without difficulty
converted into *Anarchy*. So that if anyone who is organising a
commonwealth sets up one of the three first forms of government, he sets
15 up what will last but for a while, since there are no means whereby to
prevent it passing into its contrary, on account of the likeness which in
such a case virtue has to vice. . . .
     I maintain then, that all forms of government mentioned above are far
from satisfactory, the three good ones because their life is so short, the
20 three bad ones because of their inherent malignity. Hence prudent
legislators, aware of their defects, refrained from adopting as such any one
of these forms, and chose instead one that shared in them all, since they
thought such a government would be stronger and more stable, for if in
one and the same state there was principality, aristocracy and democracy
25 each would keep watch over the other.
          Niccolò Machiavelli, *The Discourses*, c. 1519, ed. Bernard Crick,
          1970, pp 106, 109

Questions

a Define 'Aristocracy' and 'Oligarchy' (lines 11 – 12) and explain the
   difference between them.
b Do you agree that each of the three forms of 'good' government is
   very similar to the related 'bad' form?
c Explain what Machiavelli meant in the last sentence of this extract.
* d *The Discourses* imply that a republic is the best form of government.
   What events in Machiavelli's life may have led him to adopt this
   position?
* e What does this extract, together with the previous extract, suggest
   about Machiavelli as a writer on politics and government?

5 Italy in 1490

I have determined to relate the things which happened in Italy within our
memory from the time when the French armies, called in by our own
princes, began to disturb it by their great invasion. This subject, in its
variety and grandeur, is most memorable and full of the most atrocious
5 events, because for so many years Italy suffered all those calamities with
which wretched mortals are wont to be tormented, sometimes through
the just wrath of God, sometimes from the impiety and wickedness of
other men. From the knowledge of these incidents, so various and
grievous, everyone will be able to draw salutary precepts both for his
10 own and for the public good. . . .

It is clear that from the time when the Roman Empire, weakened chiefly by the change in its ancient customs, began to decline – already more than a thousand years ago – from that greatness to which it had risen by marvellous ability and fortune, Italy had never known such great prosperity nor experienced a state of affairs so desirable as that in which she rested securely in the year of our Christian salvation, 1490, and the years just before and after. In a condition of the greatest peace and tranquillity, cultivated no less in the more mountainous and arid places than in the plains and more fertile regions, not subjected to any rule except that of her own, she not only abounded in inhabitants, merchandise, and riches, but was highly renowned for the magnificence of many princes, for the splendour of many most noble and beautiful cities, for the seat and majesty of religion. She also flourished in men most distinguished in the administration of public affairs, and of noble talents in all branches of learning and in every art and skill. Since she did not lack military glory, in accordance with the custom of the age, and was adorned by such great gifts, she deservedly bore a most splendid name and fame among all the nations.

Francesco Guicciardini, *History of Italy*, 1536, in J. B. Ross and M. M. McLaughlin, *The Portable Renaissance Reader*, 1977, pp 279–80

Questions

a   Why were the French armies 'called in by our princes' (lines 2–3) and what were both the immediate and the long-term effects of the French invasion?

b   What was meant by referring to Italy as 'the seat and majesty of religion' (line 23)?

*   *c*   What was the economic basis of the idyllic picture of Italy drawn by Guicciardini?

*   *d*   Who might be included among those men 'most distinguished' in all spheres, who 'flourished' at the time of which the author was writing (lines 23–24)?

*   *e*   Do you think that people do draw 'salutary precepts' (line 9) from a knowledge of history?

6   Advice to Kings

As an intelligent and pious prince is wise, vigilant, and provident for the whole community, being one that is transacting not his own business but that of the public, so it is right that every man should endeavour to the utmost of his power to help him in his cares and anxieties; and the wider his empire, the more need has he of this kind of service. A sovereign is an exceptional being among mortals, an image of the deity; and yet he is a man. For my own part, since it is only out of my small stock of literature

that I can make payment of this duty to kings, I did some time ago turn
from Greek into Latin Plutarch's little work upon the means of
10 distinguishing a flatterer from a friend.

I have added the 'Institution of a Prince', an offering which I made not
long since to Charles, the King Catholic, when he was newly initiated
into sovereignty. Not that he stood in need of our admonitions; but, as in
a great storm, the steersman, however skilful he may be, is contented to
15 receive a warning from any quarter, so a sovereign, destined to rule so
many kingdoms, ought not to spurn any advice that is proffered in a
serious spirit, while he resolved to follow that, which of all the plans
proposed he may judge to be best. But what estuary will you anywhere
find, that has such disturbing currents as the tumults that arise in extensive
20 empires? Or who ever saw at sea such fearful tempests as those hurricanes
of human affairs, which we have witnessed in these last few years? And
still more dangerous storms appear to be impending, if things are not set
in order by the wisdom and piety of princes.

> Desiderius Erasmus, Letter to Henry VIII, from Antwerp, 9
> September 1517, in R. L. DeMolen, *Erasmus: Documents of
> Modern History*, 1973, pp 103−4

Questions

a   What does Erasmus mean by describing a sovereign as 'an image of
the deity' (line 6)?
b   Who was 'Charles, the King Catholic' (line 12) and what were the
'many kingdoms' he was 'destined to rule' (lines 15−16)?
* c   What qualities in a king does Erasmus praise in this passage? How do
these compare with the qualities advocated in extract 3?
* d   What justification does he make for his proffering of advice to rulers?
e   What 'hurricanes of human affairs' had occurred 'in these last few
years'? What much more serious 'tempest' was just about to break out
(lines 20−23)?

7   Erasmus' Defence against Charges of Lutheranism

As to Luther himself, I perceived that the better a man was the less he was
Luther's enemy. The world was sick of teaching which gave it nothing
but glosses and formulas, and was thirsting after the water of life from the
Gospels and Epistles. I approved of what seemed good in his work. I told
5 him in a letter that if he would moderate his language he might be a
shining light, and that the Pope, I did not doubt, would be his friend. . . .

I have myself simply protested against his being condemned before he
has been heard in his defence. . . .

If we want truth, every man ought to be free to say what he thinks
10 without fear. If the advocates of one side are to be rewarded with mitres
and the advocates of the other with rope or stake, truth will not be

heard. . . . Then came the terrible Bull, with the pope's name upon it. Luther's books were to be burnt, and he himself was denounced to the world as a heretic. Nothing could have been more invidious or unwise.
15 The Bull itself was unlike Leo x, and those who were sent to publish it only made matters worse. It is dangerous, however, for secular princes to oppose the papacy, and I am not likely to be braver than princes, especially when I can do nothing. The corruptions of the Roman Court may require reform, extensive and immediate, but I and the like of me are
20 not called on to take a work like that upon ourselves. I would rather see things left as they are than to see a revolution which may lead to one knows not what. Others may be martyrs if they like. I aspire to no such honour. Some hate me for being a Lutheran; some for not being a Lutheran. You may assure yourself that Erasmus has been, and always
25 will be, a faithful subject of the Roman See. But I think, and many think with me, that there would be better chance of a settlement if there was less ferocity.

Desiderius Erasmus, Letter to Lorenzo, Cardinal Campeggio, from Louvain, 6 December 1520, in *Erasmus: Documents of Modern History*, pp 129−31

Questions

a How had Erasmus tried to satisfy the world's 'thirsting after the water of life' (line 3)?

b What was the Bull? How had its publication 'made matters worse' (line 16)?

c What is Erasmus' argument in favour of free speech?

d Why does Erasmus say he has not tried to reform the Roman church, even though it needs reform?

* *e* Which of Erasmus' views, as expressed in this letter, was shared by the Emperor Charles v? How did Charles show this?

8 The Restoration of the Gospel

Why may we not aspire to see our age restored to the likeness of the primitive Church, when Christ received a purer veneration, and the splendour of His Name shone forth more widely? . . . As the light of the Gospel returns, may He Who is blessed above all grant also to us this
5 increase of faith, this purity of worship: as the light of the Gospel returns, I say, which at this time begins to shine again. By this divine light many have been so greatly illuminated that, not to speak of other benefits, from the time of Constantine, when the primitive Church, which had little by little declined, came to an end, there has not been greater knowledge of
10 languages, more extensive discovery of new lands, or wider diffusion of the name of Christ in the more distant parts of the earth than in these times.

The knowledge of languages, and especially of Latin and Greek (for afterwards the study of Hebrew letters was stimulated by Johann Reuchlin), began to return about the time when Constantinople was captured by the enemies of Christ, and when a few Greeks, notably Bessarion, Theodore of Gaza, George of Trebizond, and Manuel Chrysoloras, took refuge in Italy.

Soon afterwards the new lands were discovered, and thereupon the name of Christ was propagated [there]. . . . Would that the name of Christ might have been, and may henceforth be, proclaimed purely and sincerely so that soon the word may be fulfilled: 'O Lord, may the whole earth adore Thee'. Yes, may it offer Thee a religion evangelical and pure, a religion of the spirit and of truth! It is this above all which is to be desired.

Jacques Lefèvre d'Étaples, Commentarii initiatorii in IV evangeliis praefatio, 1522, in The Portable Renaissance Reader, pp 85–6

Questions

  a In what ways did the author wish 'to see our age restored to the likeness of the primitive Church' (lines 1–2)?

  b How far was this desire typical of the concerns of the humanists at this time?

  c For what development does the author, in effect, give credit to the enemies of Christ?

  d How effective was the propagation of the Gospel in 'the new lands' (lines 19–20)?

  e What was the importance of the author in the French church during the 1520s and 1530s?

9 The Excellence of This Age

We here in the West have in the last two hundred years recovered the excellence of good letters and brought back the study of the disciplines after they had long remained as if extinguished. The sustained industry of many learned men has led to such success that today this our age can be compared to the most learned times that ever were. For we now see the languages restored, and not only the deeds and writings of the ancients brought back to light, but also many fine things newly discovered. In this period grammar, poetry, history, rhetoric, and dialectic have been illumined. . . . Never has mathematics been so well known, nor astrology, cosmography, and navigation better understood. Physics and medicine were not in a state of better perfection among the ancient Greeks and Arabs than they are now. Arms and military instruments were never so destructive and effective, nor was there equal skill in handling them. Painting, sculpture, modelling, and architecture have been almost wholly restored. . . . Even politics, including and controll-

ing everything, which seemed to have been left behind, has recently
received much illumination. Theology, moreover, the most worthy of
all . . . has been greatly illuminated by the knowledge of Hebrew and
Greek; and the early fathers of the church, who were languishing in the
20 libraries, have been brought to light. Printing has greatly aided this work
and has made easier its development. . . .

The princes who have done most to revive the arts are Pope Nicholas v
and Alfonso King of Naples, who welcomed honourably and rewarded
liberally those who presented to them Latin translations of Greek books.
25 The King of France, Francis I, paid the salaries of public professors in
Paris, and created a sumptuous library at Fontainebleau. . . . Without
the favour and liberality of the kings of Castile and Portugal, the
discovery of the new lands and the voyage to the Indies would not have
come about. The Medici lords of Florence, Cosimo and Lorenzo, helped
30 very much, receiving the learned men who came to them from all parts,
supporting them honourably.

Loys Le Roy, *De la Vicissitude ou Variété des Choses en l'Univers*,
1575, in *The Portable Renaissance Reader*, pp 91–2, 97

Questions

a What was the significance of printing for the other developments
described by the author?
*
b Which of the various developments included in this extract were the
most important for the future?
c How important to the Renaissance was the contribution of princes,
both those mentioned and others?
*
d What criticism could be made of the marvellous state of learning, as
described by the author?

10 On Cannibals

I do not believe, from what I have been told about this people, that there
is anything barbarous or savage about them, except that we all call
barbarous anything that is contrary to our own habits. Indeed we seem to
have no other criterion of truth and reason than the type and kind of
5 opinions and customs current in the land where we live. . . . These
people are wild in the same ways as we say that fruits are wild, when
nature has produced them herself and in her ordinary way. . . .

This is a nation . . . in which there is no kind of commerce, no
knowledge of letters, no science of numbers, no title of magistrate or of
10 political superior, no habit of service, riches or poverty, no contracts, no
inheritance, no divisions of property, only leisurely occupations, no
respect for any kinship but the common ties, no clothes, no agriculture,
no metals, no use of corn or wine. The very words denoting lying,
treason, deceit, greed, envy, slander and forgiveness have never been
15 heard. . . .

It is remarkable with what obstinacy they fight their battles, which never end without great slaughter and bloodshed. As for flight and terror, they do not know what they are. . . . After treating a prisoner well for a long time, and giving him every attention he can think of, his captor
20 assembles a great company of his acquaintances . . . [and they] despatch him with their swords.

This done, they roast him, eat him all together, and send portions to their absent friends. They do not do this . . . for nourishment, . . . but as a measure of extreme vengeance. . . .
25 We are justified therefore in calling these people barbarians by reference to the laws of reason, but not in comparison with ourselves, who surpass them in every kind of barbarity. Their fighting is entirely noble and disinterested, . . . their only motive for war being the desire to display their valour.

Michel de Montaigne, *Essays*, Volume I, number 31, 1580, trans. J. M. Cohen, 1958, pp 108–14

Questions

a   The idea of the 'noble savage' was developed in the sixteenth century from contacts with the New World. How far does Montaigne's description accord with this idea?

b   Do you think that the society described here could ever have existed?

c   Do you agree with Montaigne's definition, in the first paragraph, of what is 'barbarous' to us?

* d   Can fighting ever be 'entirely noble and disinterested' (lines 27–8)?

II   The Impact of the Non-European World on Europe

Introduction

The great change in knowledge and understanding of the world between 1450 and 1550 was chiefly the result of the voyages of discovery. Better ships and techniques of navigation made exploration a safer business and discoveries were made which shattered the preconceived ideas of Europeans. It was at first impossible for them to believe that there was a whole new world across the Atlantic, but once the existence of the American continent was realised, the land was taken over, often in a brutal way, on behalf of Spain by a small group of determined men.

In the east, too, new sea routes were opened up and Portugal also acquired an empire, though it was less secure and more short-lived than that of Spain. By agreement between these two nations, the world was divided into their respective 'spheres of influence', but it was not long before other nations tried to intervene, as the Dutchman John Huyghen van Linschoten suggested (extract 4). Some tried to find alternative routes to the east. England's efforts brought her into contact with Russia, which had hitherto held aloof from all but her immediate neighbours. This unknown country also formed part of a 'new world' (extract 7).

Trade was one of the chief reasons why rulers such as Isabella of Castile, were prepared to finance exploration. Some men, like St Francis Xavier (extract 5), were concerned to convert the inhabitants of the newly discovered lands to Christianity, while others left Europe in pursuit of gold or personal power and glory. Indeed, almost all the credit for the development of overseas empires goes to a small number of brave and adventurous men.

Further Reading

G. R. Crone, *The Discovery of America* (Hamilton, 1969)

J. H. Elliott, *The Old World and the New 1492–1650* (Cambridge University Press, 1970)

J. H. Parry, *The Age of Reconnaissance* (Weidenfeld & Nicolson, 1963)

J. H. Parry, *Europe and a Wider World 1415–1715* (Hutchinson, 1966)

1 The First Report about the New World

Finally, to sum up in a few words the chief results and advantages of our
departure and speedy return, I make this promise to our most invincible
Sovereigns, that, if I am supported by some little assistance from them, I
will give them as much gold as they have need of, and in addition spices,
5 cottons, and mastic, which is found only in Chios [Dominica], and as
much aloes-wood, and as many heathen slaves as their Majesties may
choose to demand; besides these, rhubarb and other kinds of drugs, which
I think the men I left in the fort before alluded to have already
discovered. . . .

10 Although these matters are very wonderful and unheard of, they
would have been much more so if ships to a reasonable amount had been
furnished me. But what has been accomplished is great and wonderful,
and not at all proportionate to my deserts, but to the sacred Christian
faith, and to the piety and religion of our Sovereigns. For what the mind
15 of man could not compass, the spirit of God has granted to mortals. . . .

Therefore let King and Queen and Princes, and their most fortunate
realms, and all other Christian provinces, return thanks to our Lord and
Saviour Jesus Christ, who has bestowed so great a victory and reward
upon us; let there be processions and solemn sacrifices prepared; let the
20 churches be decked with festal boughs; let Christ rejoice upon earth as He
rejoices in heaven, as he foresees that so many souls of so many people
heretofore lost are to be saved; and let us be glad not only for the
exaltation of our faith, but also for the increase of temporal prosperity, in
which not only Spain, but all Christendom is about to share.

Christopher Columbus, Letter to Sanchez, the Royal Treasurer
of Spain, 1492, in L. Barnard and T. B. Hodges, *Readings in
European History*, 1958, pp 219–20

Questions

a Who were 'our most invincible Sovereigns' (lines 2–3) and why did
Columbus report his discoveries to them?
b What was the purpose of his first voyage?
* c What had he actually discovered?
d Why was his promise to supply 'heathen slaves' (line 6) to Spain
impossible to fulfil?
* e What later discovery in the New World was chiefly responsible for
'the increase of temporal prosperity in which . . . all Christendom is
about to share' (lines 23–4)? Why were the long-term effects of this
not what Columbus expected?

2 The Conquest of Peru

Then the guns were fired off, the trumpets were sounded, and the troops,
both horse and foot, sallied forth. On seeing the horses charge, many of

the Indians who were in the open space fled, and such was the force with
which they ran that they broke down part of the wall surrounding it, and
5 many fell over each other. The horsemen rode them down, killing and
wounding, and following in pursuit. The infantry made so good an
assault upon those that remained that in a short time most of them were
put to the sword. The Governor still held Atabaliba [Atahualpa] by the
arm. . . . During the whole time no Indian raised his arms against a
10 Spaniard. So great was the terror of the Indians at seeing the Governor
force his way through them, at hearing the fire of the artillery, and
beholding the charging of the horses, a thing never before heard of, that
they thought more of flying to save their lives than of fighting. . . .
   The Governor presently ordered native clothes to be brought, and
15 when Atabaliba was dressed, he made him sit near him, and soothed his
rage and agitation at finding himself so quickly fallen from his high estate.
Among many other things, the Governor said to him: 'Do not take it as
an insult that you have been defeated and taken prisoner, for with the
Christians who came with me, though so few in number, I have
20 conquered greater kingdoms than yours, and have defeated other more
powerful lords than you, imposing upon them the dominion of the
Emperor, whose vassal I am, and who is King of Spain and of the
universal world. We come to conquer this land by his command, that all
may come to a knowledge of God, and of His Holy Catholic Faith; and
25 by reason of our good object, God, the Creator of heaven and earth and of
all things in them, permits this, in order that you may know him, and
come out from the bestial and diabolical life you lead.'
   From a report by Veres, the Governor's Secretary, 1533, in
   C. H. Markham, *Reports on the Discovery of Peru*, 1872, pp
   55−6

Questions

a Who was the Governor and who was his employer, the King of
   Spain?
*
b Some men genuinely wanted to spread Christianity to the New
   World, but what other aims motivated most of the Spanish?
c What practices of the Incas could lead to the description of their
   'bestial and diabolical life' (line 27)?
d How far were the Governor's boasts justified by his actual
   achievements?
*
e How far do the events described in this extract foreshadow the future
   treatment of the Indians by the Spanish?

3 Potosí

The famous mountain of Potosi, at the foot of which on the south side
stands the town of the same name, is known all over the commercial

world, as having been greatly enriched by the silver it produces. The discovery of these immense mines happened in the year 1545, by an accident seemingly fortuitous. An Indian, by some called Gualca, and by others Hualpa, pursuing some wild goats up this mountain, and coming to a part very steep, he laid hold of a small shrub in order to climb it with the greater celerity; but the shrub being unable to support his weight came up by the roots, and discovered a mass of fine silver, and at the same time he found some lumps of the same metal among the clods, which adhered to the roots.

Another article of great consequence, is the trade of quicksilver for the use of these mines; but this branch the crown has reserved to itself . . . the immense consumption of quicksilver in the mines of this mountain, and the riches extracted from it, will best appear from the following. . . . Don Gaspar de Escalona . . . declares, from very good authority, that before the year 1638, it appeared by the public accounts, that the produce of the silver amounted to 395,619,000 dollars. Hence an idea may be formed of the vast commerce which has for many years been carried on in this town, and which is still like to continue for a long time.

> *A Voyage to South America*: describing at large the Spanish Cities, Towns, Provinces, etc. on that extensive continent; undertaken, by command of the King of Spain, by Don George Juan and Don Antonio de Ulloa, Captains of the Spanish Navy, 1749, in Margaret Shennan, *The European Dynamic*, 1976, pp 125−6

Questions

a Where was Potosí?

b What was the importance of quicksilver for the production of silver and what problems were involved in transporting the silver to Europe?

* c How did the kings of Spain benefit directly from the discovery of silver?

* d What effects did its export to Europe have on the economies of (i) Spain and (ii) other countries?

4 The Portuguese Empire

Mozambique is a very great and safe haven, fit to receive and harbour all ships that come and go both to and from Portugal and the Indies . . . there is also a castle wherein the Portuguese keep garrison, from whence also all other castles and forts thereabouts are supplied with their necessaries, especially Sofala, where the rich mine of Gold lies . . . which lies between Mozambique and the Cape de Bona Speranza. . . . From Mozambique they carry into India gold, ambergris, ebony wood and ivory and many slaves both men and women. . . .

The coast of Malabar [has] . . . great quantity of pepper, for that they

10 are able every year to load a ship with seven or eight thousand quintals of
pepper, Portuguese weight. . . .
    Among these Malabars the white Moors do inhabit that believe in
Mahomet, and their greatest traffic is to the Red Sea, although they may
not do it, neither any Indian, without the Portuguese passport, otherwise
15 the Portuguese army (which yearly sails along the coasts, to keep them
clear from sea rovers) for the safety of their merchants, finding them or
any other Indian or nation at sea without a passport, would take them for
a prize. . . .
    South southeast right over against the last point of the Ile of
20 Sumatra . . . lies the island called Java Major, or great Java, where there is
a straight or narrow passage between Sumatra and Java called the straight
of Sunda. . . . Some think [Java] to be firm land (and parcel) of the
country called Terra Incognita, which (being so) should reach from that
place to the Cape of Good Hope, but as yet it is not certainly known, and
25 therefore it is accounted for an island. . . . In this place of Sunda there is
much pepper . . . it has likewise much frankincense, . . . camphor, also
diamonds; to which place men might very well traffic, without any
impeachment, for that the Portuguese come not thither, because great
numbers of Java come themselves to Malacca to sell their wares.
        The Voyage of John Huyghen van Linschoten to the East Indies,
        English translation of 1598, in Margaret Shennan, *The European
        Dynamic*, 1976, pp 91–4

Questions

a Where are Mozambique, the coast of Malabar and Malacca? What
   was 'Terra Incognita' (line 23)?
b Why was Mozambique very important to Portuguese sailors?
c Against which nation was Portuguese control of the Red Sea
   directed? Why did Portugal want to maintain this control?
* d In what sense is the last sentence prophetic?
* e How had it been possible for the Portuguese to acquire an empire in
   the East without interference from other European powers? Why did
   it collapse so easily?

5 A Christian Missionary in Japan

By the experience which we have of this land of Japan, I can inform you
thereof as follows. Firstly, the people whom we have met so far are the
best who have yet been discovered, and it seems to me that we shall never
find among heathens another race to equal the Japanese. . . . This land of
5 Japan is very fit for our holy faith greatly to increase therein; and if we
knew how to speak the language I have no doubt whatsoever that we
would soon make many Christians. May it please Our Lord that we may
learn it soon, for already we begin to appreciate it. . . . What we in these

parts endeavour to do, is to bring people to the knowledge of their
10 Creator and Saviour, Jesus Christ our Lord. We live with great hope and
trust in Him to give us strength, grace, help and favour to prosecute this
work. . . . They cannot do us more harm than God permits, and what
harm comes to us through them is a mercy of God; if through them for
His love, service and zeal for souls, He sees good to shorten the days of our
15 life, in order to end this continual death in which we live, our desires will
be speedily fulfilled and we will go to reign forever with Christ. Our
intentions are to proclaim and maintain the truth, however much they
may contradict us, since God compels us to seek rather the salvation of
our future than the safety of our present lives; we endeavouring with the
20 grace and favour of Our Lord to fulfil this precept, He giving us internal
strength to manifest the same before the innumerable idolatries which
there are in Japan.

> St Francis Xavier, letter to the Jesuits in Goa, from Kagoshima,
> Japan, 5 November 1549, in C. R. Boxer, *The Christian Century
> in Japan, 1549–1650*, 1951, pp 401–14

Questions

a Under the auspices of which European organisation had St Francis
   Xavier gone to Japan?
*
b Which other countries did he visit in the Far East and what success did
   he have there?
c What were the author's aims, for himself and for the Japanese, in
   going to Japan?
d Suggest why St Francis viewed his mission with such optimism. Was
   his optimism justified?
*
e What were the aims of the Society of which St Francis was a member?
   Why did few of its members follow him to the Far East?

6   Problems for Venice

[The] King of Portugal sent with the . . . ships money to the value of
60,000 ducats provided by the aforesaid king and other merchants for this
voyage to India. . . . I can say for the profit, that from one ducat they can
make more than one hundred. . . . And if this voyage should con-
5 tinue . . . the King of Portugal could call himself the King of Money
because all would convene to that country to obtain spices, and the
money would accumulate greatly in Portugal with such profit as would
follow each year from similar voyages. When this news was truly learned
in Venice, the whole city was much stirred by it, and everyone was
10 stupefied that in this our time there should have been found a new voyage
which was never heard of or seen in the time of the ancients or of our
ancestors. And this news was held by the learned to be the worst news
which the Venetian Republic could have had. . . . There is no doubt

whatever that the city of Venice came to such reputation and fame as it
15 now enjoys only through the sea, namely by the continual traffic and
navigations which it has made by the voyages, because they carry each
year a large quantity of spices with their galleys and ships so that very
great damage would be done to deprive them of it. . . .

Because the spices which come to Venice pass through all of Syria and
20 through all of the countries in the Venetian state they pay insufferable
duties, presents and excises. . . . Therefore . . . whatever costs a ducat
would be multiplied in price . . . to the amount of sixty or one hundred
ducats. . . .

Therefore the King of Portugal, having found this voyage the other
25 way round, would alone have the spices of the caravels, which they
would import for much less in comparison with the other spices
mentioned above, and for this reason they could give the spices a much
better market than can the Venetian merchants.

> Letter of Il Cretico, Venetian nuncio to Portugal, 1501, in
> Margaret Shennan, *The European Dynamic*, 1976, pp 172–3

Questions

a What were the chief spices brought to Europe from India? Why was there a considerable demand for them in Europe?
* b What were the main differences between galleys and caravels?
* c By what route did Venice acquire spices? Why was this route both dangerous and expensive?
d What does the writer mean by 'this voyage the other way round' (lines 24–5)?
* e What was the importance, for the future of Venice, of Portugal's entry into the spice trade?

7 Chancellor's Voyage to Muscovy

On being admitted . . . into the Presence Chamber, the wondrous
display of Imperial splendour was such as quite dazzled the eyes of our
men. For they saw the Emperor of the Russians seated aloft upon his
throne, conspicuous to all eyes by the golden diadem on his brow,
5 wearing the robe of State, a marvellous product of workmanship in gold,
and holding in his right hand a golden sceptre, embellished with gems.
But apart from all these insignia of his sovereign wealth, there was at
the same time a majesty in his looks worthy of his exalted
position. . . . Chancellor . . . having paid his respects to the Emperor
10 according to the fashion of the English court, delivered the letter of King
Edward. When this had been read, the Emperor asked briefly as to the
king's health. The English replied (in accordance with what they hoped)
that he was well and alive. Immediately on this a present was offered to
the Emperor by our men. . . .

15 The Emperor, whenever his rights are infringed by his neighbours, never arms against the enemy a host under 900,000 strong. From this number he leads out for active service 300,000 men, and distributes the rest for garrison-duty into places conveniently situated for the defence of the Empire. He chooses his soldiery neither from the agricultural nor
20 trading classes, for so great is the multitude of his subjects, that apart from these, the teeming population furnishes abundance of young recruits for his wars. . . .

If the prince has been energetically assisted in war by any one, he presents that person with his maintenance, or with a piece of land for the
25 support of himself and his family, but this land reverts to the Emperor himself, should it so happen that the beneficiary has no male children. . . . Moreover, he who is rewarded in this manner by the Imperial munificence, is bound under a heavy pecuniary penalty, to rear as many soldiers for war, ready to take the field when necessity requires, as the
30 revenue of that domain can easily support, according to an estimate made by the Emperor.

Clement Adam, *Anglorum Navigatio ad Muscovitas*, 1886, taken from *Respublica Muscoviae*, 1630

Questions

a Who was 'the Emperor of the Russians' (line 3)?
b What was the purpose of Chancellor's visit? How successful was he?
c Who were the 'neighbours' (line 15) who might infringe the rights of the Emperor? What did the Emperor gain from his wars against them?
*
d In what way, in the middle years of his reign, did the Emperor upset the system of landholding described here? Why did he do this and what were the results?
*
e What aspects of the Emperor's rule would not be apparent to visitors such as Chancellor?

8 The Assimilation of Discoveries

The main and ultimate object of the discoverers was to reach inhabited places on the far coasts of . . . the tripartite land-mass of Europe, Asia and Africa which, for most mediaeval cosmographers, was all the world that existed. The last thing they expected to find . . . was an intervening
5 continent. . . .

The discoverers . . . were initially very reluctant to accept the full implications of what they found; to understand that a new, separate landmass of vast and unknown extent must be added to the map of the world. Such a land-mass, if it existed, would be a contradiction of accepted
10 geographical authority. It would be a severe commercial disappointment, an obstacle to cherished hopes. It would be, moreover, a challenge to

faith. The new lands were inhabited. Were Christian Europeans to believe that a whole branch of the human race had lived, perhaps since the Creation, separated from the rest of mankind, cut off from the possibility
15 of redemption, not, as Muslims were, by contumacy and diabolical misdirection, but cut off by hard physical fact? The implications were profoundly disturbing; it is not surprising that many informed Europeans were slow to accept them. A whole generation of explorers and geographers tried, by any arguments they could find, to fit America-to-
20 be into the accepted pattern of the world; to suggest a connection between the new lands and distant parts of the *orbis terrarum*, which they had not seen but which they had heard of or read about. There is an ambiguity in many contemporary narratives, descriptions and maps which makes it difficult to define in precise modern terms what the
25 explorers were looking for and what they thought they had found. In common phrases such as 'new land', 'new country', even 'new world' . . ., 'new' certainly meant new to Europeans, but it did not necessarily mean unheard-of. It was not until Magellan had revealed the daunting size of the Pacific, and Cortes had discovered the wealth and
30 complexity of Mexican society, that the informed in Europe accepted America unequivocally as a wholly new continent, of wide interest and promise in its own right.

J. H. Parry, *The Discovery of South America*, 1979, pp 23−5

Questions

a Why did Europeans find it so difficult to accept the evidence of America as a separate continent?

b How did some people try to make it fit into their preconceived ideas?

* *c* Why was the discovery both 'a commercial disappointment' (line 10) and 'a challenge to faith' (lines 11−12)?

* *d* Whose discoveries helped to make the idea of America acceptable? Why was this?

9 The Old World and the New

America impinged on sixteenth- and early seventeenth-century Europe at innumerable points. Its discovery had important *intellectual* consequences, in that it brought Europeans into contact with new lands and people, and in so doing challenged a number of traditional European
5 assumptions about geography, theology, history and the nature of man. America also constituted an *economic* challenge for Europe, in that it proved to be at once a source of supply for produce and for objects for which there existed a European demand, and a promising field for the extension of European business enterprise. Finally, the acquisition by
10 European states of lands and resources in America was bound to have important *political* repercussions, in that it affected their mutual relations by bringing about changes in the balance of power. . . .

'It is a striking fact,' wrote the Parisian lawyer, Etienne Pasquier, in the early 1560s, 'that our classical authors had no knowledge of all this America, which we call New Lands.' With these words he caught something of the importance of America for the Europe of his day. Here was a totally new phenomenon, quite outside the range of Europe's accumulated experience and of its normal expectation. Europeans knew something, however vaguely and inaccurately, about Africa and Asia. But about America and its inhabitants they knew nothing. It was this which differentiated the response of sixteenth-century Europeans to America from that of the fifteenth-century Portuguese to Africa. The nature of the Africans was known, at least in a general way. That of the Americans was not. The very fact of America's existence, and of its gradual revelation as an entity in its own right, rather than as an extension of Asia, constituted a challenge to a whole body of traditional assumptions, beliefs and attitudes. The sheer immensity of this challenge goes a long way towards explaining one of the most striking features of sixteenth-century intellectual history – the apparent slowness of Europe in making the mental adjustments required to incorporate America within its field of vision.

> J. H. Elliott, *The Old World and the New 1492–1650*, 1970, pp 6–8

Questions

a Which 'traditional European assumptions about geography' (lines 4–5) were challenged by the discovery of America?

b In what other ways did the discovery have 'intellectual consequences' (lines 2–3)?

*
c What 'objects for which there existed a European demand' (lines 7–8) were found in America? What effects did this increased supply
*
have?

d What might Europeans have known 'vaguely and inaccurately' about Africa and Asia (line 19)? What were the sources of their knowledge?

10 The Business of Exploration

Vespucci returned to Spain in 1505. . . . His work was significant not only because of the extent of his discoveries, not only because of the publicity – unsought by him – which they received, but even more because of the soundness of his geographical knowledge and judgment. As an interpreter of discoveries he was unsurpassed.

After him all Europe recognised America for what it was, a new continent and a barrier – to everyone except the Portuguese, an unwelcome barrier – between Europe and Asia. The problem of finding a western passage to the spice islands, therefore, became not a problem of

10   threading a way through an archipelago of islands, but one of finding a
strait through a land mass whose dimensions from east to west were
unknown. . . .
     Almost every European monarch at one time or another dreamed of
finding a western passage and breaking the Portuguese monopoly of
15   eastern trade. This universal ambition called for a new type of specialist —
the professional explorer. The exploring activity of the early sixteenth
century was dominated by a small group of men whose national
allegiance sat lightly upon them and who were qualified and willing to
undertake exploration on behalf of any monarch who would employ
20   them. . . . Most of them were Italians, such as Vespucci himself,
Verrazano and the two Cabots, father and son, or Portuguese such as
Fernandes, Magellan and Solís. They served in turn the Kings of Spain,
France and England and the Grand Signory of Venice. Against a
background of growing jealousies and diplomatic cross-purposes they
25   changed allegiances at will and carried from court to court information
which their employers would have preferred to keep secret; yet such was
the value set upon their knowledge that they were always welcome
wherever they chose to settle. Only the Portuguese took care to employ
their own nationals wherever they could; and consequently only the
30   Portuguese succeeded in keeping their discoveries secret.
     J. H. Parry, *Europe and a Wider World 1415 – 1715*, 1966, pp 48 – 9

Questions

a   Where had Vespucci's expeditions taken him?
b   Why was America regarded as an 'unwelcome barrier' (line 8) by
       everyone except the Portuguese?
*   *c*   By what right had Portugal established a 'monopoly of eastern trade'
       (lines 14 – 15)?
d   Why should the employers of the 'professional explorers' (line 16)
       have wished to keep their discoveries secret?
*   *e*   What were the chief motives behind the great interest in exploration
       from the 1480s onwards?

III Charles V

Introduction

Charles V ruled a vast empire, covering large areas of Europe, and even larger areas of America were added to it during his lifetime. Gradually he came to realise that it was too much for one man and so he divided his lands between his son and his brother at the end of his life. The sheer size of his empire meant that, unlike a modern ruler, he could not attempt to rule it all effectively himself, even though he travelled a great deal. There was no attempt to impose a uniform system of government throughout his lands, such a thing being inconceivable in the sixteenth century, although there was a regular way of doing business at the centre (extract 3). The problems which faced Charles during his reign were daunting — rebellions, political (as in Spain), economic and religious (as in the Netherlands and Germany), and external enemies, such as France and the Ottoman empire, threatening his lands.

Charles himself found his position difficult and, in general, thought long and hard before taking any action. It can be argued that he had no very positive policies, but instead reacted to events without trying to impose his own pattern on them. Certainly in foreign affairs the constant attacks by France, at least until 1529, left little opportunity for initiatives in other areas. Some contemporaries would have been inclined to defend and approve him, as did the Venetian ambassador in 1551 (extract 4), rather than attack him vehemently as did the nineteenth-century American historian, J. L. Motley (extract 8).

Charles' most serious problem was the internal one posed by Luther, because Charles believed that his position as emperor imposed on him the duty to defend Christendom. This is considered in section V.

Further Reading

Mañuel Fernández Alvarez, *Charles V* (Thames & Hudson, 1975)
Karl Brandi, *Charles V* (Cape, 1968)
J. H. Elliott, *Imperial Spain 1469—1716* (Edward Arnold, 1963)
John Lynch, *Spain under the Hapsburgs* (Oxford, Blackwell, 1964—9)
Maurice Rowdon, *The Spanish Terror* (Constable, 1974)

1 Charles Takes Stock of his Position

When I sat down to think out my position, I saw that the first thing at
which I must aim and the best that God could send me, was peace. Peace is
beautiful to talk of but difficult to have, for as everyone knows it cannot
be had without the enemy's consent. I must therefore make great
5   efforts – and that, too, is easier said than done. . . .

A successful war may help me. But I cannot support my army, let alone
increase it. . . . My friends have forsaken me in my evil hour; all are
equally determined to prevent me from growing more powerful and to
keep me in my present distressed state.

10 Furthermore, the armies are now very close to one another. A battle in
which I shall be either victorious or wholly defeated cannot be postponed
for much longer. . . .

I can think of no better way in which to improve my condition than by
going myself to Italy.

15 Doubts may be raised because of the money needed, or because of the
regency in Spain, or on other grounds. In order to overcome these
difficulties I think the best way would be to hurry on my marriage to the
Infanta of Portugal and to bring her here as soon as possible. For the
money which is to be sent with her is a very large sum in actual
20 bullion. . . . But my marriage will be a good reason to demand a great
sum of money from the Spanish kingdoms. I shall have to call and
dissolve the Cortes to achieve this. The Infanta of Portugal, who by that
time will be my wife, must be appointed regent of these kingdoms, to
rule them well according to the good advice of those I shall leave with
25 her.

In this way I ought to be able to set out for Italy with the greatest
splendour and honour in this very autumn.

Private memorandum by Charles v, January 1525, in K. Brandi,
The Emperor Charles v, trans. C. V. Wedgwood, 1968, pp
219–21

Questions

a   Who was 'the enemy' (line 4)? Where were the armies 'very close to
one another' (line 10)?

b   What happened soon after Charles wrote this note, to change the
whole situation?

c   Why might he have been right to suppose that even his friends were
'determined to prevent me from growing more powerful' (line 8)?

*
d   Why was the regency in Spain a problem? How had Charles solved
the problem of his absence from his other lands?

*
e   What was the Cortes? Had Charles reason to seem slightly apprehen-
sive about calling it?

*
f   How much of this programme did Charles actually put into effect?

2 The Demands of the German Peasants

1 It is our humble request and prayer, and also our general desire and intent, that in future we shall have power and authority for every congregation to elect and choose its own minister. . . . The said minister so chosen shall preach the holy gospel purely and clearly without any
5 additions made by man, teach us the true faith, give us cause to ask God for His grace, and erect and confirm the true faith in us. . . .

2 Where the tithe is ordained in the Old Testament and released in the New, nevertheless we will gladly pay the proper tithe of corn, but only in due manner. Each man shall give to God and shall share his own with a
10 true minister who preaches the word of God. . . .

3 It has been the custom hitherto to hold us for bondmen, which is a pitiful matter, seeing that Christ with His precious blood has freed and bought us all, the hind as well as the highest, no man excepted. Therefore we assert that we are free and will be free; not that we wish to be free
15 altogether and renounce all authority. . . . God's command does not show and order us to refuse obedience to lordship; we are to be humble not only towards lordship but towards all men and to obey our chosen and appointed superiors (if appointed by God) in all proper and Christian matters. . . .

20 6 We complain most heavily about the labour services which are daily increased and daily grow. We demand that this be looked to and that we be not so burdened beyond measure.

From the Twelve Articles agreed by the German peasants at Memmingen, 1525, in G. R. Elton, *Renaissance and Reformation 1300–1648*, 1976, pp 324–5

Questions

a What did the peasants mean by 'true faith' (line 5)?
b What is 'the tithe' (line 7)? What, by implication from article 2, was the peasants' objection to the demands for tithes being imposed on them?
* c Which of Luther's doctrines was behind the demand in article 3? In what way did Luther think this doctrine was misinterpreted by the peasants? What effect did Luther's reaction have on the peasants and their beliefs?
d What were 'labour services' (line 20)?
* e To which group of lords were the peasants most strongly opposed?
* f What were the long-term effects of the revolt?

3 Charles v's System of Government

The affairs which pertain to business are divided in this way. His Majesty has three chancelleries which always follow the court, with a secretary in chief for each and many lesser officials and scribes. The first is that of the

Empire, through which pass all the documents and affairs of Germany
5 and Italy that are dependent upon it; the second is the Spanish, which
settles the affairs of Spain and the Indies; the third is that of Naples and
Sicily, and this one also has the responsibility of the concessions of favours
that are commonly made. All these affairs are settled after infinite delay
and length of time.
10   Then there is another separate set of treasurers or exchangers who are
trained in accounts, and with the advice of some of these his Majesty
borrows money on the exchange and at interest, and thus makes
provision for whatever he needs in time of war and peace. And it is
remarkable that although in the past wars they have borrowed at from
15 ten up to twenty-five and thirty per cent yearly, the emperor has never
wished to fail in his word to the merchants. The result is that if he has
indeed suffered some inconvenience, he has, nevertheless, so well
preserved his credit that in any great war which might occur the
merchants would never fail him. Such a thing is of the greatest
20 importance to a prince, in my opinion, because in any case of need he can
say that he has in reserve as much money as he wants.
    For the government of his states his Majesty maintains a council made
up of various experienced regents, one for Sicily, one for Naples, one for
Milan, one for Burgundy, one for the Low Countries, one for Aragon
25 and one for Castile, with two or three other experts, who all together, in
matters of highest importance, consult and pass judgment on every
concern of the emperor which pertains to the states.
        From the report of Marino Cavalli, Venetian ambassador, 1551,
        in *The Portable Renaissance Reader*, pp 298−9

Questions

a Why were affairs only settled 'after infinite delay and length of time'
   (lines 8−9)?
* b What were the main sources from which Charles borrowed money
   and what was the ultimate effect on them of this borrowing?
* c The council of regents travelled with Charles, but how were his
   various lands actually governed during his absence?
* d This account implies that the system applied in the same way to all
   Charles' lands. How far did he pursue a policy of uniformity and why
   was this generally unsuccessful?

4 A Complimentary Assessment of Charles v

The emperor is now fifty-one years of age, in ill health because of the
gout, which distresses him terribly all winter and sometimes at other
seasons. . . .
    But when his Majesty was in sound health he was most accomplished in
5 all bodily exercises and a most excellent horseman. . . . He has as great a

knowledge of horses, of artillery, of quartering armies, of storming cities, and of every detail pertaining to war as any man alive today, and not only on land but also in matters of the sea. He uses great care in understanding every detail of his affairs. . . .

10 His Majesty is very religious; he hears two Masses every day; . . . and in the public eye he lives like a Christian, in private like a knight. He has no defects at all because he abstains from all vices; and in all his actions, even the most trivial, he is so well composed and ordered, so well informed and so judicious that no one could desire more; with certain

15 gestures and certain words so prudent that they deserve to be admired by everyone. He always speaks kindly, never grows angry or threatens, but always with justice in his mouth, with hope in God, and founding his policies on legal right. . . .

He is not bloodthirsty or revengeful to the point of seeking the utter

20 ruin of his enemies; he weakens but does not destroy them. . . . He is extremely well informed, and secretly, from all sides; he discusses affairs four or five hours continuously at a time, sitting on a chair, and sometimes he writes down the reasons for and against a point in order to see better how it is reasoned. He deliberates slowly and is then resolute.

From the report of Marino Cavalli, Venetian ambassador, 1551, in *The Portable Renaissance Reader*, pp 300–302

Questions

a Where had Charles' personal mastery of matters 'pertaining to war' resulted in great victories (line 7)?

*

b The author says that Charles 'has no defects at all' (line 12), but what were his chief faults or weaknesses?

*

c Give at least one example of Charles' attempts to weaken but not to destroy his enemies. Were there any occasions when his policy was one of destruction and was this more successful?

d Which of the virtues the ambassador attributes to Charles are the most valuable for a ruler?

*

e Do you think that this account is fairer to Charles than is extract 9?

5 Part of Charles v's Abdication Speech

Although [my councillor] Philibert has just fully explained to you, my friends, the causes which have determined me to surrender the possession and administration of these Belgian provinces and leave them to my son, Don Philip, yet I wish to say certain things with my own mouth. You

5 will remember that upon the fifth of January of this year there had elapsed forty years since my grandfather, the emperor Maximilian, in the same place and at the same hour, declared my majority at the age of fifteen, withdrew me from the guardianship under which I had remained up to that time, and made me master of myself. . . .

10   Soon came the death of my grandfather Maximilian, in my nineteenth
year, and although I was still young I sought and obtained the imperial
dignity in his stead. I had no inordinate ambition to rule a multitude of
kingdoms, but merely desired to secure the welfare and prosperity of
Germany, my dear fatherland, and of my other kingdoms, especially of
15   my Belgian provinces; and to encourage and extend as far as in me lay
Christian peace and harmony throughout the whole world.
    But although such zeal was mine, I was unable to show so much of it as
I might have wished, on account of the troubles raised by the heresies of
Luther and the other innovators of Germany, and on account of serious
20   war into which the hostility and envy of neighbouring princes had driven
me, but from which I have safely emerged, thanks to the favour of
God. . . .
    I am determined then to retire to Spain and to yield to my son Philip
the possession of all my Belgian provinces. I particularly commend my
25   son to you, and I ask of you, in remembrance of me, that you extend to
him the love which you have always borne towards me. . . . Be just and
zealous in the observance of the laws, . . . and do not refuse to grant to
authority the support of which it stands in need. Above all, beware of
infection from the sects of neighbouring lands.
    Charles v, at Brussels, 25 October 1555, in J. H. Robinson,
    Readings in European History, vol II, 1906, pp 165 – 7

Questions

a   Had Charles ruled 'a multitude of kingdoms' (lines 12 – 13)? Why did
he have a special feeling for his Belgian provinces?
b   Would you agree that Charles showed 'no inordinate ambition' (line
12) and that his troubles were not of his own making?
c   How far was it true that Charles' lands had, by 1555, 'safely emerged'
from the 'serious war' in which they had been involved (lines 19 – 21)?
*
d   Comment on the last paragraph in the light of subsequent events.
*
e   Why had Charles taken the unprecedented decision to abdicate?

6   Heresy in Spain

I am very satisfied with what you say you have written to the king
informing him of what is happening about the people imprisoned as
Lutherans, more of whom are being daily discovered. But believe me,
my daughter, this business has caused and still causes me more anxiety and
5   pain than I can express, for while the king and I were abroad these realms
remained in perfect peace, free from this calamity, but now that I have
returned here to rest and recuperate and serve Our Lord, this great
outrage and treachery, implicating such notable persons, occurs in my
presence and in yours. . . . Since this affair is more important for the
10   service of Our Lord and the good and preservation of these realms than

any other, and since it is only in its beginnings, with such small forces that they can be easily put down, it is necessary to place the greatest stress and weight on a quick remedy and exemplary punishment. I do not know whether it will be enough in these cases to follow the usual practice, by which according to common law all those who beg for mercy and have their confession accepted are pardoned with a light penance if it is a first offence. Such people, if set free, are at liberty to commit the same offence, particularly if they are educated persons. . . .

It is clear that they cannot act without armed organisation and leaders, and so it must be seen whether they can be proceeded against as creators of sedition, upheaval, riots and disturbance in the state; they would then be guilty of rebellion and could not expect any mercy. . . . [In Flanders] I wanted to introduce an Inquisition to punish the heresies that some people had caught from neighbouring Germany and England and even France. Everyone opposed this on the grounds that there were no Jews among them. . . .

Believe me, my daughter, if so great an evil is not suppressed and remedied without distinction of persons from the very beginning, I cannot promise that the king or anyone else will be in a position to do it afterwards.

Charles v, letter to his daughter Juana, regent of Spain, 25 May 1558, in H. Kamen, *The Spanish Inquisition*, 1965, pp 85—6

Questions

a   Who was 'the king' (line 1) and why did he need a regent at this time?
b   Explain Charles' statement 'I have returned here to rest and recuperate and serve Our Lord' (lines 6—7).
c   What is the significance of the reference to the Jews?
* d   Why do you think Charles' final paragraph is pessimistic in tone? Was this pessimism justified by subsequent events in Spain?
* e   Why had the Spanish Inquisition originally been set up? How far was its existence responsible for the failure of Protestantism to become established in Spain?

7   An Unfortunate Start

The court made a ceremonial entry into Valladolid, meaning again to blind the Spanish with splendour. . . .

[Charles'] advisers kept Spanish ministers away from him as much as they could. He made his first mistake by giving Spanish bishoprics to Burgundians. . . .

The demands made of the king by the Cortes of Castile in 1518 were amazing for their sense of independence. . . . Charles v swore respect for Castilian rights, in return for recognition as king. It was only the first lesson.

10   Other demands followed. The Cortes laid it down that no more
benefices should be given to foreigners. . . . The king himself must learn
Spanish and hold a daily audience. He should keep a firm hand on the
Inquisition, and see that confiscated property did not go to the judges
who confiscated it. Also there must be a sufficient number of witnesses for
15   an indictment of heresy to be made. The king was advised to marry at
once, and, it was demanded, his younger brother Ferdinand should not
leave Spain until Charles's queen had had a child. . . . The Burgundians
returned polite answers to most of these demands, and got the money
they were asking for (600,000 ducats).
20   With the money in his pocket Charles moved on to Aragon. It was his
second big mistake to spend more time there and in Catalonia than he had
done in Castile. . . . He started off by vowing to respect Aragonese
liberties but very soon realised that almost nobody looked on him as their
protector anyway. His mother (most Aragonese seemed not to know that
25   she was incurably mad) and his younger brother were preferred almost
unanimously. . . .
    The emperor Maximilian died in 1519. In the short term Charles's
desire to take his place aggravated the Spanish situation. . . . The rumour
got round that Charles would soon be leaving. Spaniards began to feel
30   that they had put up money to benefit policies not their own. Again there
would be a regent, this time a foreigner, Adrian of Utrecht.
    Maurice Rowdon, *The Spanish Terror*, 1974, pp 72−5

Questions

a   Who are meant by the 'Burgundians' (line 5)?
b   Why did the people of Aragon prefer Charles' mother and his
    younger brother?
*   *c*   How many of the demands of the Cortes of Castile did Charles, in
    time, accede to?
*   *d*   Explain what Charles' mistakes were and why appointing a foreigner
    as regent was another mistake. Why did Charles make such an
    unfortunate start? How did the opposition to him show itself?
*   *e*   In what ways did Charles make up for this unfortunate start, during
    the rest of his reign?

8   A Hostile Assessment of Charles v

His conduct towards [the Netherlands] during his whole career had been
one of unmitigated oppression. . . . The interests of the Netherlands had
never been even a secondary consideration with their master. He had
fulfilled no duty towards them, he had committed the gravest crimes
5   against them. He had regarded them merely as a treasury upon which to
draw; while the sums which he had extorted were spent upon ceaseless
and senseless wars, which were of no more interest to them than if they

had been waged in another planet. Of five millions of gold annually, which he derived from all his realms, two millions came from these industrious and opulent provinces. . . . The rivalry of the houses of Habsburg and Valois, this was the absorbing theme. . . . To gain the empire over Francis, to leave to Don Philip a richer heritage than the Dauphin could expect, were the great motives of the unparalleled energy displayed by Charles during the longer and the more successful portion of his career. To crush the Reformation throughout his dominions, was his occupation afterward, till he abandoned the field in despair. It was certainly not desirable for the Netherlanders that they should be thus controlled by a man who forced them to contribute so largely to the success of schemes, some of which were at best indifferent, and others entirely odious to them. . . .

But if his sins against the Netherlands had been only those of financial and political oppression, it would be at least conceivable although certainly not commendable, that the inhabitants should have regretted his departure. But there are far darker crimes for which he stands arraigned at the bar of history. . . . His hand planted the inquisition in the Netherlands. . . . The number of Netherlanders who were burned, strangled, beheaded, or buried alive, in obedience to his edicts, and for the offences of reading the Scriptures, of looking askance at a graven image, or of ridiculing the actual presence of the body and blood of Christ in a wafer, have been placed as high as one thousand by distinguished authorities.

> J. L. Motley, *The Rise of the Dutch Republic*, vol I, 1862, pp 101 – 103

Questions

a What were the sources of wealth of 'these industrious and opulent provinces' (line 10)?

b What effect did Charles' constant financial demands of them eventually have?

c Against which group, in particular, was the inquisition's work directed at this time? How successful was it?

d How much of the author's criticism of Charles seems to you to be justified? Which parts of it are unjustifiable?

e Can you find in the text any indications of the reason why the author feels so vehemently critical of Charles?

9 Charles v's Character and Place in History

Charles v carried the Hapsburg dynasty to the height of its greatness. He united and completed its possessions; mingling old Burgundian ideas of chivalry with the conscientious piety of the Netherlands, with Spanish self-restraint and the universal traditions of the Romano–German

5　Empire, he created the attitude which was in future to be typical of his dynasty. At the same time, out of the mass of his inherited possessions he formed a new European, and, in a sense, a new overseas imperialism – a world Empire dependent for the first time in history not on conquest, still less on geographical interdependence, but on dynastic theory and unity of
10　faith.

The Emperor gave his Empire not only new foundations but new ambitions, which found expression in the conflict in the Netherlands, and in the wars in Germany, Italy and Spain.

On the younger branch of the dynasty he bestowed the old rights over
15　the Danube lands, with their important possibilities and no less important dangers, while he shifted the weight of his own power from Germany and Burgundy to the growing state of Spain. Thus he founded within his own family that predominance of the Spanish branch which lasted for a century and a half. Resting not on Germany, but on Spain, he was able to
20　reassert his suzerainty over the old imperial lands of Milan, Tuscany, and even Naples; thereby he turned the axis of the Empire, which had run for so long from north to south, on to the line of Madrid and Rome, and sheltered Italy for many years to come from the attacks of France. Basing his imperial theory on Spain, he regained both for himself and his son that
25　relationship with the Papacy as an Italian power within the framework of the European system, which had prevailed during the earlier days of the Empire. For reasons rooted deep in German history his relations with the Protestants were governed at least as much by political as by ecclesiastical considerations. In his world-struggle for the ancient Church, the
30　Emperor was to experience the bitter mortification of being deserted by the Pope, and he was to be touched to the quick by the alliance of Catholic France with the Turk. . . .

The same latent tension is to be found in internal politics. Inevitably Charles's highly centralized policy over-rode the individual territorial
35　divisions of his lands; thereby he weaned them from outworn political forms based on disintegrating feudal and urban authority, with their special privileges, local feuds and shifting powers, and drew them towards higher political conceptions. . . . The Emperor's dynastic policy of world-power gave rise to the ideas prevalent in Europe during the
40　century which saw the rise of the nation-state, a direction which survives to-day. . . .

Many as are the seeming contradictions in the life of Charles v it had an inner unity. His career was dominated by the dynastic principle, which found more vital and effective expression in him than in any other ruler in
45　the history of the world. Both as a man and as a sovereign, he was subjected to the moral pressure of this principle, which beset his path with perilous temptations. The Emperor gave living reality in his own person to the doctrine of a binding relationship between the generations, of responsibility alike towards his ancestors and his descendants. For him the
50　dynastic principle did not merely mean the theory of hereditary kingship for the permanent security of the state; it was also a profound moral,

almost a religious duty. Charles was not indeed unlike other princes of his time in his physical weaknesses; but he was far above them all in the political sanctification, as it were, of his marriage, in the courtly and
55 princely reverence which he showed to his wife, Her Serene Majesty, the Empress. No father could have displayed greater care for the spiritual and material welfare of his children than this Emperor who, in the forty years of his reign, wandered ceaselessly from land to land, waged war after war, negotiated treaty after treaty, and spent in all that time hardly one
60 continuous year by his own fireside.

> Karl Brandi, *The Emperor Charles V*, trans. C. V. Wedgwood, 1968, pp 13−16

Questions

a   Explain the references to Burgundy and 'the younger branch of the dynasty' (line 14).

b   Do you agree that Charles 'turned the axis of the Empire . . . on to the line of Madrid and Rome' (lines 21−2)?

c   Were Charles' relations with the Protestants 'governed at least as much by political as by ecclesiastical considerations' (lines 28−29)?

*

d   How far did Charles succeed, as the author suggests, in centralising control of all his lands?

*

e   What does the author mean by 'the dynastic principle' (line 43) and what was its chief expression among his descendants?

f   What are the chief characteristics of Charles which emerge from this extract?

IV   The New Monarchy

Introduction

'The new monarchy' is a useful phrase to describe the kind of monarchy which developed at the end of the fifteenth and the beginning of the sixteenth centuries. This was a time when rulers all over Europe were extending their authority and exercising greater power over their subjects. The church, the army, taxation, legislation, all had a part in this development. In a limited space it is not possible to examine all the rulers of the time, so here the emphasis is on France, with two extracts (numbers 9 and 10) to illustrate what was happening elsewhere.

Francis I of France carried this new style of government as far as it was possible to do at the time and had more absolute power than any of his rivals, although his constant wars were damaging to his country and developments in France in the second half of the century showed how greatly this kind of rule depended on the personality of the monarch. How absolute Francis actually was is a matter of opinion. Claude de Seyssel's book was concerned to make clear the extent, as well as the limitations, of the king's power (extract 3), but not all historians would accept that the king of France was as absolute as Seyssel believed.

Another characteristic of these 'new monarchs' was that they were well educated and knowledgeable about the cultural and artistic fashions of the day. Many of them were patrons of the arts; Francis I is a good example of this too. He persuaded Leonardo da Vinci to spend his last years in France and employed a number of other artists, as well as Benvenuto Cellini, the most famous goldsmith of the day (extract 6).

Further Reading

(Ed.) A. G. Dickens, *The Courts of Europe* (Thames & Hudson, 1977)

Lucien Febvre, *Life in Renaissance France* (Harvard University Press, 1978)

Desmond Seward, *Prince of the Renaissance* (Constable, 1973)

J. H. Shennan, *The Origins of the Modern European State 1450−1725* (Hutchinson, 1974)

(Ed.) J. M. Wallace-Hadrill & J. McManners, *France: Government and Society* (Methuen, 1957)

1 'The New Monarchy'

An outstanding development in the complex pattern of sixteenth-
century Europe was the growth of a number of vigorous monarchical
states, each seeking an efficient machinery of centralised administration,
proud of its independence and eager to further its dynastic interests. . . .

5   At the risk of over-simplification some listing of the typical marks of
these new monarchies may be attempted. They were seated in a definite
territory; and their subjects tended to have a common language, a
common outlook, a common pride and common ideals. At least in
embryo there existed what we have come to call nationalism. The rulers
10 leaned . . . toward authoritarianism and therefore faced a possible
challenge in the various representative bodies or estates of which the
medieval period had so many examples. For various reasons kings were in
need of larger revenues, the customary sources of which — income from
the royal domains, customs, tolls, occasional special levies and the like —
15 proved in most cases to be no longer adequate. A tendency arose,
therefore, for royal power to assert itself in the financial realm against
what the medieval world had looked upon as the property rights of the
subject. . . .
    With all this came an increased royal regulation of economic life upon
20 a nation-wide scale. The slow standardization of the coinage, the more
efficient and uniform collection of taxes, the granting of charters for
exploration, trade and settlement, the regulation of imports and of
domestic manufacture and sale — in short, the conscious direction of
economic life in the interests of the state — were diverse aspects and
25 beginnings of what later came to be known as mercantilism. This
vigorous assertion of national economic interests was one of the forces
helping to create more ambitious and more militant foreign policies. . . .
    In the opening decades of the sixteenth century nothing is more
striking than the way in which a splendid cast of royal figures dominated
30 the European stage. Not only were their aims and methods very similar,
but each also seemed to embody in his person something of the state over
which he ruled. . . . The outstanding examples were found in Spain,
England and France.

       E. J. Knapton, *Europe 1450–1815*, 1958, pp 80–4

Questions

a   In what ways did the 'new monarchs' try to further their 'dynastic
    interests' (line 4)?
b   In which countries was there the strongest challenge to the ruler from
    'the various representative bodies' (line 11)?
c   Why did royal incomes so often prove 'to be no longer adequate' (line
    15)?
d   What was the importance of 'charters for exploration' (lines 21–2)
    and which kings benefited from granting them?
e   Which rulers of the period seem best to fit the picture drawn in this

extract? In what sense can it be claimed that the early sixteenth century was 'dominated' by 'a splendid cast of royal figures' (line 29)?

2 Princes and Parliaments

By the end of the fifteenth century the balance of social and political forces was changing enough to affect significantly the relationships between princes and parliaments. . . . In western Europe, conditions were favourable for the development of strong monarchies in the early
5 sixteenth century. The monarchies of England, France and Spain had all emerged victorious from civil war with overmighty subjects. Even before the Reformation they had established themselves as the dominant partners in their alliance with the Church, for example in the appointment of bishops, the levy of taxation from the clergy, and the pursuit of
10 heretics. They had succeeded in making the monarchy militarily stronger than any internal force, and though this tempted them into adventures abroad, they were able to keep solvent by a variety of financial expedients, ranging from sale of offices and revival of feudal dues to loans and taxes. They were able to insist on their sole control of foreign policy
15 and even to take a greater initiative in legislation.

But the Reformation, contrary to what is often thought, tended for a time to make the monarchy more dependent on the cooperation of the estates. The Spanish monarchy found itself increasingly involved in wars against the Protestant powers and the Turks, and in most of its dominions
20 had to appeal to the local parliament — whether in Aragon, Sicily, Naples or the Netherlands — for increased financial aid. In this matter Castile was a conspicuous exception. In France, the monarchy, which had not summoned a full Estates–General since 1484, had to hold a series of meetings to attempt to deal with religious strife. . . .
25 In the Protestant states of Germany, the Reformation was carried out by the prince, and the bishops disappeared as an independent force; but through financial necessity most princes had to sell the Church lands quickly and then turn to the *Landtag* for money to protect them from Catholic attack. The *Landtag* used the opportunity to gain fresh privileges
30 and some say in church affairs.

> A. R. Myers, *Parliaments and Estates in Europe to 1789*, 1975, pp 148–52

Questions

a How far does this description fit any one prince of the early sixteenth century in his relations with his parliament?
b How had it been possible for these rulers to become 'the dominant partners in their alliance with the Church' (lines 7–8)?
c Were 'adventures abroad' (lines 11–12) important to all the rulers of this time? Which of them particularly succumbed to this temptation?

* d   What was the the political position of many German bishops around
        1500? What happened as a result of the Reformation?
* e   What was the position of most of these parliaments in 1600?

3   Francis I of France as an Absolute Monarch

The authority and power of the king in France is regulated and restrained
by three checks . . . the first is Religion, the second Justice and the third,
Police. . . .

5   With regard to the first, it is an indisputable fact that the French have
always been, and still are, . . . pious and God-fearing. . . . For that
reason it is both proper and necessary that whoever is king should make it
known to the people by example and by visible and outward signs that he
is a zealot, an observer of the Faith and of the Christian religion, and that
he is resolved to use his power to sustain and strengthen it . . . so long as
10   the king respects . . . the Christian religion he cannot act as a tyrant.

Justice, which is the second check . . . indubitably carries more weight
in France than in any other country in the world, especially because of the
institutions of the *Parlements*, whose principal role is to bridle the absolute
power which kings might seek to use. . . . In the matter of distributive
15   justice the king has always been subject to these courts, so that in civil
cases an individual may gain satisfaction and justice indiscriminately
against the king or against his subjects. . . . Besides, justice is that much
more powerful because those who are deputed to administer it have
permanent possession of their offices and the king has no power to
20   remove them, save in the event of forfeiture . . . .

The third check is that of Police, by which is intended those many
ordinances that have been promulgated, and subsequently confirmed and
approved from time to time, by the kings themselves, which help to
preserve the kingdom as a whole and the rights of the individuals who
25   compose it.

> Claude de Seyssel, *La Monarchie de France*, 1515, in J. H. Shennan,
> *Government and Society in France 1461 – 1661*, 1969, pp 77 – 8

Questions

a   Explain how the religion of the king acts as a check on his power.
b   How could the *Parlements* 'bridle the absolute power which kings
    might seek to use' (lines 13 – 14)? Was the *Parlement* of Paris able to
    do this effectively? What other functions did it have?
c   How did the administrators of justice obtain 'permanent possession of
    their offices' (line 19)? What were the disadvantages of this?
d   How would you describe the third check on the king's authority?
* e   What other checks, in law or practice, were there on Francis I's
        powers?
* f   What is meant by 'an absolute monarch'? How far is this a true
        description of Francis?

4 The Concordat of Bologna

With the advice and unanimous approval of our brothers, with our
certain knowledge and full authority, we hereby enact and ordain that
henceforth and for ever in the future in place of the pragmatic sanction or
constitution and of each and every chapter contained therein, the
5 following shall be observed:
Henceforward, in the case of vacancies now and in the future in
cathedral and metropolitan churches of the said kingdom [of
France] . . . whoever is king of France shall within six months counting
from the day on which the vacancy occurred present and nominate to us
10 and to our successors, as bishops of Rome or to the apostolic see to be
invested by us, a sober or knowledgeable master or graduate in theology,
or a doctor or graduate in all or in one of the laws taught and rigorously
examined at a famous university, who must be at least twenty-seven years
old and otherwise suitable. . . .
15 Given at Rome at a public assembly held in the holy consecrated
church of the Lateran, in the year of Our Lord 1516, the 14th day of
January and the fourth year of our Pontificate. . . .
Wherefore our dear and well-beloved councillors at present and in the
future members of our *parlements* and all judges in our kingdom . . . and
20 other officers and subjects are commanded and charged, to the extent that
each is involved, closely to maintain, respect and observe all the above-
mentioned decisions.
Recital of Concordat issued by Francis I at Paris, 13 May 1517, in
J. H. Shennan, *Government and Society in France 1461 – 1661*, 1969,
pp 85 – 6

Questions

a   Which pope issued this Concordat? Why did he feel he must make
concessions at the time to the king of France?
b   What was the 'pragmatic sanction' (line 3) which was superseded by
this agreement?
c   Why did the king need to submit the Concordat to the 'members of
our *parlements*' (line 19), and what was their reaction?
*   d   What other aspects of relations between church and state were
covered by the agreement?
*   e   What were the advantages which Francis gained from this
agreement?

5 Taxation in France

Francis, by the grace of God, king of France, to all those who will see
these letters, greetings. For the defence, protection and safeguarding of
our kingdom, territories, lands and *seigneuries* and in order to resist and
hinder the enterprises of our enemies against the kingdom and Crown of

France, our royal predecessors have seen fit to raise and maintain a large body of soldiers. In order to pay them and to bear the other great expenses, burdens and needs which the incidence of war has forced them to support and sustain, our predecessors have been compelled to augment and multiply the impositions, *aides, tailles* . . . and *gabelles*. According to the ordinances of our predecessors concerning the *aides* and *gabelles* all manner of men are liable, except those who are specifically exempted by the ordinances, and therefore they ought to bring in a great deal of revenue; however, it has been brought to our notice that some of our subjects, almost the majority, of various conditions, even the richest and most affluent, have violated these ordinances in attempting every day to gain exemption, to plunder and defraud us of the taxes and funds due to us from the said *aides* and *gabelles*, diminishing our revenue to such an extent that there is good reason — and we might be obliged hereafter — to increase the burden on our wretched people, especially by means of the *taille*, to our very great regret, sorrow and affliction, for with all our heart and might we desire to relieve them and preserve them from exactions and oppression. . . . We ordain that all towns, places, colleges, communities, our officers and other individuals shall be subject to payment of the *tailles*, the strong supporting the weak, with the exception of those who by royal ordinance or by special immunity duly confirmed, verified and drawn up by us are exempt and may enjoy their exemption fully and peacefully.

An Ordinance concerning taxation, issued by Francis I, 1517, in J. H. Shennan, *Government and Society in France 1461 – 1661*, 1969, pp 142 – 4

Questions

a Which country or countries would Francis have regarded as 'enemies against the kingdom' (line 4)?

b What 'great expenses' (lines 6 – 7) were incurred by war, apart from paying the troops?

c What were (i) '*tailles*' and (ii) '*gabelles*' (line 9)?

d Why was the *taille* an especial 'burden on our wretched people' (line 19)? Who had the right not to pay it?

* e Was it possible for this ordinance to be effectively enforced?

6 A Visitor to the French Court, 1540

We found the King's court at Fontainebleau, where we presented ourselves to the Cardinal who immediately found us quarters; and for that night we were very comfortably placed. Next morning the little cart arrived. We secured our belongings, and when the Cardinal heard of this he told the King, who at once wanted to see me. I went to his Majesty, taking the bowl and jug with me, and when I entered his presence I kissed

his knee and he received me very graciously. I thanked his Majesty for having freed me from prison, saying that a prince such as his Majesty, a man of his unique goodness, was bound to liberate men who had some
10 talent, and especially innocent men like me, and that such generous deeds were written down in God's book, ranking higher than anything else.

That good king listened till I had finished, behaving with great courtesy, and interposing a few words typical of his fine nature. When I had come to an end he took the bowl and jug and said:
15 'I am certain that such beautiful work was never known to the ancients: I well remember having seen all the best works done by the finest craftsmen of all Italy, but I never saw any that moved me more than this'. . . .

Then [the King] turned to me and said in Italian:
20 'Benvenuto, spend a few days enjoying yourself, set your mind at rest and have a good time. Meanwhile we shall plan how to let you have all you need to start on some fine work for us.' . . .

At this time we were following the court, or rather, struggling along behind, because the King's train always drags along behind it twelve
25 thousand horsemen; in peace-time when the court is complete there are eighteen thousand, and so with twelve thousand the number is at its lowest. So there we were, following the court through places where sometimes there were scarcely two houses to be seen. We pitched canvas tents like the gipsies; and more than once we had to suffer great
30 discomfort.

Benvenuto Cellini, *Autobiography*, 1558, trans. G. Bull, 1956, pp 251–2

Questions

a When had Francis I had the opportunity to see 'the best works . . . of all Italy' (lines 16–17)?
* b Why did the king travel round the country so much? What were the advantages of this constant movement?
* c What kind of people travelled in his immense train?
d What qualities of Francis I are illustrated by this extract? What does it reveal of the author's character?

7 Was Francis I an Absolute Monarch?

[A] brief survey of the reign of Francis I has produced little evidence to support the view that the monarchy of Renaissance France was 'popular and consultative' rather than absolute. If we take the line that absolutism precludes any form of consultation, any ceiling to the amount of taxation
5 which can be realistically exacted, and any dependence on the support of a powerful social group, then clearly Francis I was not absolute. But has any ruler in history, however authoritarian, ever fulfilled these exacting

criteria? Absolutism in practice has always fallen short of its theoretical completeness and Francis would appear to have been about as absolute as any European monarch of his day could ever hope to be. He . . . never showed the slightest inclination to take advice from a circle wider than his own council. . . . Francis 1's fiscal exactions won him the international reputation of being a tyrant. His attempt to extend the *gabelle* to the provinces of the south-west in 1542 provoked a serious rebellion which had to be put down by force. The king's religious policy also derived from his authoritarianism for he would not accept any definition of heresy other than his own. His attempt to distinguish between evangelical humanists and Lutherans, whilst laudable in itself, was doomed to fail from the start. By his inability to pursue a clear course of action either for or against the Reformation until 1534 Francis paved the way for the violent troubles of the future. In this way and also by his abuse of the venality of offices, which created a kind of 'fourth estate' with interests of its own, he helped to undermine royal authority in the long term. . . . His reign witnessed a considerable expansion of the royal domain, the creation of a more manageable fiscal administration, the establishment of closer links between the central government and the provinces, the continued codification of French customary law and the completion of the linguistic unification of the kingdom.

R. J. Knecht, *Francis 1 and Absolute Monarchy*, 1969, pp 28–9

Questions

a What is meant by 'venality of offices' (line 22)? What was the advantage of the system to the king?

b Why did Francis wish to 'distinguish between evangelical humanists and Lutherans' (lines 17–18)? Why was the policy 'doomed to fail from the start' (lines 18–19)?

* c Describe the membership and responsibilities of Francis's council.

d What was the importance for France of the 'codification of French customary law' and 'linguistic unification' (lines 27–8)?

* e How did Francis 'undermine royal authority in the long term' (lines 23–4)?

* f Do you agree that Francis was 'about as absolute as any European monarch of his day could ever hope to be' (lines 9–10)?

8 Henry II Asks for Money, 1552

The king . . . issued letters-patent addressed to his trusty and well-beloved Jean de Tignac, lieutenant-general of the seneschalcy of Lyons, instructing him to convene the estates of Dombes at Trévoux, to ask from them a free gift of 10,000 *livres* like the one which they had granted to his father, Francis I, in 1542. . . . Monsieur de Tignac came to Trévoux on the fourteenth of June, having summoned the representatives of the three

estates in the customary fashion. . . . Monsieur de Tignac informed them
of the king's intentions and of his need for funds and exhorted them to
agree to the imposition of the 10,000 *livres* which the king was asking for.
10 The deputies gave their opinions in the absence of Monsieur de Tignac.
The Sire Varinier and the nobles were in favour of making the gift.
Monsieur Nicole Melier replied for the third estate, arguing that in the
past no more than two or three thousand *livres* had been granted and such
grants had been delayed for two or three years; that 10,000 *livres* had
15 never been granted and that the area was so poor that it would be difficult
to find this amount in this year. He requested that the gift should be made
in two payments, half in the current year and half in the following year.
But after hearing Monsieur de Tignac's account of His Majesty's
pressing needs it was agreed to pay the whole amount together.

> J. H. Shennan, *Government and Society in France 1461 – 1661*, 1969,
> pp 122 – 3

Questions

a What were the 'three estates' (lines 6 – 7)?
* b What could have happened had the estates refused to agree to this
grant? Why was it unlikely that Monsieur Melier's suggestions would
be accepted?
c Why did Henry II have 'pressing needs' (line 19) for money at this
time?
* d Why were only some areas of France consulted about taxation in this
way and which areas were they?

9 King Henry VIII of England

His Majesty is twenty-nine years old and extremely handsome; nature
could not have done more for him. He is much handsomer than any other
sovereign in Christendom; and a great deal handsomer than the king of
France; very fair, and his whole frame admirably proportioned. . . . He
5 is very accomplished, a good musician, composes well, is a most capital
horseman, a fine jouster, speaks good French, Latin and Spanish; is very
religious – hears three masses daily when he hunts, and sometimes five on
other days. . . .
He is very fond of hunting, and never takes his diversion without tiring
10 eight or ten horses. . . . He is extremely fond of tennis, at which game it
is the prettiest thing in the world to see him play. . . .
He is affable and gracious, harms no one, does not covet his
neighbour's goods, and is satisfied with his own dominions, having often
said to me, 'Sir ambassador, we want all potentates to content themselves
15 with their own territories; we are satisfied with this island of ours.' He
seems extremely desirous of peace.
He is very rich. His father left him ten millions of ready money in gold,

of which he is supposed to have spent one half in the war against
France. . . .

20   The cardinal of York is of low origin. . . . He rules both the king and
the entire kingdom. On my first arrival in England he used to say to me,
'His Majesty will do so and so.' Subsequently, by degrees, he forgot
himself, and commenced saying, 'We shall do so and so.' At this present
he has reached such a pitch that he says, 'I shall do so and so.' He is about
25   forty-six years old, very handsome, learned, extremely eloquent, of vast
ability, and indefatigable. He alone transacts as much business as that
which occupies all the magistracies, offices, and councils of Venice, both
civil and criminal; and all state affairs likewise are managed by him, let
their nature be what it may.
             Report of the Venetian ambassador, Giustiniani, 1519, in J. H.
             Robinson, *Readings in European History*, vol II, 1906, pp 137—8

Questions

a   What evidence is there in this extract that Henry VIII had been
      educated to fit the Renaissance ideal of a prince?
b   Would you agree that Henry was 'very religious' (lines 6—7)? In what
      ways had his interest in religion shown itself by 1535?
c   Was Henry sincere in disclaiming territorial ambitions? Why, then,
      had he recently been to war against France?
d   Who was the cardinal of York? What does it suggest about Henry's
      character that the cardinal had been able to acquire so much power?
*   *e*   How do Henry's position and power compare with those of Francis I?
f   To what extent was the ambassador's flattering account a reliable
      report of Henry and his minister?

10   The Ordinance of Västeras, 1544

First, that the Word of God and Holy Scripture shall generally be used in
the Christian congregation here in Sweden.
2 It is forbidden to worship or pray to departed saints. . . .
5 The common people shall attend in church during the hours of
5   worship. . . .
9 Our gracious lord the king, the Council of the whole realm, the
nobility, bishops, prelates, muncipalities and commons have taken oath
that they will never depart from the doctrine now established. . . .
13 The king's son, Duke Eric, has been chosen, approved and elected by
10   the commons to be the future king of the realm of Sweden, and his
descendants after him, one after another. . . .
15 His grace has sworn never to seek anything but the good, the profit
and the well-being of Sweden.
16 His grace has proclaimed peace within the realm and outside it.
15   17 The whole realm have promised that if treason be discovered in the
kingdom they will themselves punish and suppress it.

18 The commons have sworn fealty, submission, loyalty and service in war to our gracious lord. . . .

24 Our gracious lord and the commons of the realm have agreed that
20 anyone contravening this ordinance and thereof convicted by two witnesses shall be outlawed and held to be an heretic and infidel.

G. R. Elton, *Renaissance and Reformation 1300–1648*, 1976, pp 211–12

Questions

a Which king of Sweden issued this ordinance to complete the Reformation in his country?

b What is there in the wording or tone of the ordinance to indicate that the Reformation introduced a form of Lutheranism into Sweden?

c Why was it necessary to settle the succession to the throne in clause 13?

d Why was it so important to associate the commons with the king's decisions?

e What do clauses 15 – 18 suggest about the recent history of Sweden? What had the king already achieved in the twenty-one years of his reign? Does he deserve to be described as a 'new monarch'?

V   The German Reformation

Introduction

To contemporaries Luther's sudden appearance on the scene in 1517 seemed startling and unlikely to have any permanent effect. Looking back from a distance of more than four hundred years it is possible to see Luther as the culmination of growing opposition to the church. German nationalism was roused by demands for papal taxation and local anticlericalism by the only too apparent faults of some priests who expected special treatment and privileges and contributed little to the community. The development of printing enabled Luther's ideas to spread rapidly to all parts of Germany, though they were not always fully understood, as the demands of the rebellious peasants of 1524–6 showed (extract 2 in section III).

The pope and Charles V condemned Luther (extract 3), but at the same time there were attempts to reconcile him to Rome and to other protestant leaders, notably Zwingli at Marburg in 1529 (extract 7). Many of the German cities were attracted by his ideas and adopted them (extract 4), but this did not always cause a permanent break with Rome. It was in states such as Saxony where the ruler adopted Lutheranism, that it became most securely established and was given legal approval by the Peace of Augsburg (extract 8).

Further Reading

Roland H. Bainton, *Here I Stand* (Hodder & Stoughton, 1950)
A. G. Dickens, *Martin Luther and the Reformation* (Hodder & Stoughton, 1977)
A. G. Dickens, *The German Nation and Martin Luther* (Edward Arnold, 1974)
V. H. H. Green, *Luther and the Reformation* (New English Library, 1974)
Hans J. Hillerbrand, *The World of the Reformation* (Dent, 1975)
(Ed.) Joel Hurstfield, *The Reformation Crisis* (Edward Arnold, 1965)

1   An Attack on Indulgences

To the Right Reverend Father in Christ, Lord Albrecht, Archbishop of Magdeburg and Mainz, his esteemed lord and shepherd in Christ. May the Grace of God be with him.

May your Electoral Highness graciously permit me, the least and most
unworthy of men, to address you. . . .

With your Electoral Highness's consent, the Papal Indulgence for the
rebuilding of St. Peter's in Rome is being carried through the land. I do
not complain so much of the loud cry of the preacher of Indulgences,
which I have not heard, but regret the false meaning which the simple
folk attach to it, the poor souls believing that when they have purchased
such letters they have secured their salvation, also, that the moment the
money jingles in the box souls are delivered from purgatory, and that all
sins will be forgiven through a letter of Indulgence, even that of reviling
the blessed mother of God, were any one blasphemous enough to do so.
And, lastly, that through these Indulgences the man is freed from all
penalties! Ah, dear God! Thus are those souls which have been committed
to your care, dear Father, being led in the paths of death, and for them
you will be required to render an account. . . .

How then can you, through false promises of Indulgences, which do
not promote the salvation or sanctification of their souls, lead the people
into carnal security, by declaring them free from the painful consequences of their wrong-doing with which the Church was wont to
punish their sins?

For deeds of piety and love are infinitely better than Indulgences, and
yet the bishops do not preach these so earnestly, although it is their
principal duty to proclaim the love of Christ to their people. Christ has
nowhere commanded Indulgences to be preached, only the Gospel.

Luther, from Wittenberg, 31 October 1517, in E. G. Rupp and
B. Drewery, *Luther: Documents of Modern History*, 1970, pp 17–
18

Questions

a   Why should Luther address a letter against Indulgences to Albrecht,
archbishop of Mainz? Why does Luther address him as 'your Electoral
Highness' (line 4)?
b   Explain the official purpose of Indulgences.
c   What 'false promises' (line 19) does Luther suggest are being made by
the sellers of Indulgences?
*
d   How did Luther's opposition to the sale of Indulgences lead
ultimately to his breaking away from the catholic church?
*
e   What other reasons were there for his opposition to official
catholicism?

2   'Concerning Christian Liberty'

One thing, and one alone, is necessary for life, justification and Christian
liberty; and that is the most holy word of God, the Gospel of Christ. . . .
Let us therefore hold it for certain and firmly established that the soul

can do without everything except the word of God, without which none
5 at all of its wants are provided for. But, having the word, it is rich and
wants for nothing. . . .

Hence it is clear that as the soul needs the word alone for life and
justification, so it is justified by faith alone, and not by any works. . . .

Nor are we only kings and the freest of all men, but also priests for ever,
10 a dignity far higher than kingship, because by that priesthood we are
worthy to appear before God, to pray for others, and to teach one another
mutually the things which are of God. For these are the duties of priests,
and they cannot possibly be permitted to any unbeliever. Christ has
obtained for us this favour, if we believe in him. . . .

15   As then trees must exist before their fruit, and as the fruit does not make
the tree either good or bad, but, on the contrary, a tree of either kind
produces fruit of the same kind, so must first the person of the man be
good or bad before he can do either a good or a bad work; and his works
do not make him bad or good, but he himself makes his works either bad
20 or good. . . .

We do not then reject good works; nay, we embrace them and teach
them in the highest degree. It is not on their own account that we
condemn them, but on account of this impious addition to them and the
perverse notion of seeking justification by them.

Martin Luther, 'Concerning Christian Liberty', 1520, in E. G.
Rupp and B. Drewery, *Luther: Documents of Modern History*,
1970, pp 51−3

Questions

a What did Luther mean by the phrases 'justified by faith' (line 8) and
'good works' (line 21)?

b What does Luther say are the duties of a priest and how did his
understanding of the priesthood differ from that of the catholic
church?

c What was Luther's attitude to 'good works', as partly explained in the
last paragraph of this extract?

* d What did Luther mean by 'Christian liberty' (lines 1−2)? Why did he
regard it as so important that it provided the title for this pamphlet?

3   The Edict of Worms, May 1521

Charles v, . . . emperor . . . , to the electors, princes, etc., one and all,
greetings and blessings. . . .

None of you can be in any doubt how far the errors and heresies which
a certain Martin Luther, of the Augustinian order, seeks to disseminate,
5 depart from the Christian way. . . .

Hence it is our duty to proceed against this festering disease as follows:
First: to the praise and glory of Almighty God and the defence of the

Christian faith and the honour due to the Pontiff and See of Rome — and furthermore with the unanimous agreement and wish of our own and the Holy Empire's electors, princes and orders now gathered in this place — we pronounce and declare that the said Martin Luther shall be held in detestation by us and each and all of you as a limb severed from the Church of God, the author of a pernicious schism, a manifest and obstinate heretic; and this we do in order that the whole business may never be forgotten, and that the decree, sentence and condemnation in the Bull, which our Holy Father the Pope issued in his capacity as Judge Ordinary of religious controversies, may be put into effect. . . .

Our strict order . . . is that after the appointed twenty days . . . you shall refuse the aforesaid Martin Luther hospitality, lodging and bed; that none shall feed and nourish him with food or drink, or assist and further him by the counsel and help of word or deed, secretly or openly; but wherever you meet him, if you have sufficient force, you shall take him prisoner. . . .

As for the books of Martin Luther which our Holy Father the Pope has condemned, as well as any of his many other writings, in German or Latin, . . . we order that nobody shall henceforth dare to buy, sell, keep, copy, print or cause them to be copied and printed, or approve his opinions, or support, preach, defend or assert them in any way. . . . For they are impious, foul, suspect, half-baked, the work of a notorious and persistent heretic.

E. G. Rupp and B. Drewery, *Luther: Documents of Modern History*, 1970, pp 61 – 2

Questions

* *a* What was the Augustinian order and what was its significance in Luther's life?
 b What was the 'sentence and condemnation in the Bull' (lines 15 – 16) issued by the pope?
 c For what reasons was Luther offered 'hospitality' (line 19) by the Elector of Saxony after he left Worms?
* *d* What difference might it have made to the progress of the Reformation in Germany if it had been possible to enforce the emperor's ban on the circulation of Luther's writings?

4   Strassburg Accepts the Reformation, 1524

At this stage no less than five of the nine Strassburg city parishes spontaneously drew up a petition to the council which forms something of a landmark. It is a rather fumbling document but it vividly reflects the attitudes of laymen stimulated by Protestant sermonizing. These parishioners drew up a sharp antithesis between the ignorant old priest and the educated preacher. They say they must have such preachers because

they themselves, their wives and children cannot otherwise attain the Word of God. . . . The parishes could already boast a supply of university-trained clerics and should be taken over by the city. Then, in
10 alarmingly secular terms, the parishioners grumble that they have to work hard every weekday and do not want their Sunday quiet to be disturbed by ecclesiastical pageantry or by what they call 'the unnecessary howling of choirs'. *Bürgerlich* peace and unity, they add, would be restored by the appointment of godly preachers, who could be supported
15 by a careful management of the old parish endowments, and would not necessitate new taxation. . . .

Thus encouraged by pressure from below, the council now assumed the right of appointing to parish incumbencies on the grounds that the old patrons . . . had not done their duty, that disorder had developed, and
20 that the parishioners themselves were forcibly installing preachers. The magistrates also ruled that, on appointment, new incumbents must swear loyalty to the city and the council. Characteristically their official edict says nothing about doctrine, not even about the 'pure Word of God'. . . . One of the vital changes had occurred: a cautious and still
25 divided city council had placated Protestant parishioners and, without tarrying overmuch for theology, had taken steps to establish Protestant teaching in the parishes. The council had indeed become an accomplice of the Reformers; it had assumed ecclesiastical functions which its members or their successors would never be likely to renounce. . . . Whatever
30 steps Protestant theology had failed to inspire had been suggested by the instinct of laymen to enlarge state-sovereignty at the expense of the Church. As events were soon to show, that instinct had become endemic throughout Europe.

A. G. Dickens, *The German Nation and Martin Luther*, 1974, pp 151–2'

Questions

a What were the parishioners of Strassburg asking for in their petition?
b Why do you think the author refers to the 'alarmingly secular terms' (line 10) of part of this petition?
c Why should the city council make new incumbents swear loyalty to the city and itself?
*
d Why do you think the council did not specify the doctrine to be taught and how had the position changed thirty years later?
e In what way did the council 'enlarge state-sovereignty' (line 31)?
*
f The Reformation lasted in Strassburg; why was it less successful in establishing itself in some other German cities?

5 Of Magistrates

I have thought it particularly desirable to include a discussion of magistrates, and first, for pedagogic reasons, I shall follow the usual classification. Magistrates are held to be divided into civil and ecclesiastical. A civil magistrate is he who possesses the sword and preserves the civil peace. . . .

Concerning the exercise of this power of the sword I hold as follows:

One, if princes command anything contrary to God this is not to be obeyed. . . .

Two, if they command anything arising out of the public interest this must be obeyed. . . .

Lastly, if any of their commands are tyrannical, here too the magistrate is to be suffered for charity's sake in all cases where change is impossible without public commotion or sedition. . . .

My views of ecclesiastical magistrates are these: in the first place bishops are ministers, not potentates or rulers. Next, they have no right to make laws, having but a mandate to preach the Word of God. . . .

Christ dispensed from the traditions of the Pharisees; but from the civil law he did not dispense. . . . The administration of all human laws involves faith and charity and also necessity. This frees us from all traditions in every instance in which either the soul or the life of the body may by a tradition be brought into peril.

Philip Melanchthon, *Loci Communes*, 1521, in G. R. Elton, *Renaissance and Reformation 1300–1648*, 1976, pp 188–90

Questions

a What does the author mean here by 'magistrates' (line 2)? Why should this name be used in this context?

*
b What was Luther's attitude, shared by Melanchthon, to relations between church and state? How did this compare with the views of other protestant reformers of the sixteenth century?

c With what in this extract would the Roman Catholic church have disagreed?

*
d What was Melanchthon's importance to the development of Lutheranism in the sixteenth century?

6 Erasmus' Criticism of Luther

I do not object generally to the evangelical doctrines, but there is much in Luther's teachings which I dislike. He runs everything which he touches into extravagance. True, Christendom is corrupt and needs the rod, but it would be better, in my opinion, if we could have the pope and the princes on our side. . . . Clement was not opposed to reform, but when I urged that we should meet him half-way nobody listened. The violent party carries all before it. They tear the hoods off monks who might as well have been left in their cells. Priests are married, and images are torn down. I would have had religion purified without destroying authority. Licence

10 need not be given to sin. Practices grown corrupt by long usage might be
gradually corrected without throwing everything into confusion. Luther
sees certain things to be wrong, and in flying blindly at them causes them
more harm than he cures. Order human beings as you will, there will still
be faults enough, and there are remedies worse than the dis-
15 ease. . . . Would that Luther had tried as hard to improve popes and
princes as to expose their faults. . . .

   You are anxious that Luther shall answer me with moderation. Unless
he write in his own style, the world will say we are in connivance. Do not
fear that I shall oppose evangelical truth. I left many faults in him
20 unnoticed lest I should injure the Gospel. I hope mankind will be the
better for the acrid medicines with which he has dosed them. Perhaps we
needed a surgeon who would use knife and cautery. Carlstadt and he are
going so fast that Luther himself may come to regret popes and
bishops. . . . The devil is a clever fellow. Success like Luther's might spoil
25 the most modest of men.

Erasmus, Letter to Philip Melanchthon, from Basle, 10 December
1524, in R. L. DeMolen, *Erasmus: Documents of Modern History*,
1973, pp 149–50

Questions

a By using the phrase 'on our side' (line 5), Erasmus implies that he and
Luther have the same aim. What does the passage suggest that this aim
was?

b What is Erasmus' chief criticism of Luther? How far was this justified?

c Why does Erasmus not wish to be answered 'with moderation' by
Luther (line 17)?

*

d Who was Carlstadt? What does Erasmus mean by the sentence about
Carlstadt and Luther? How did the relationship between them
develop after 1524?

7 The Marburg Conference, 1529

The landgrave [of Hesse] decided that there should be separate pre-
liminary conferences in private, Oecolampadius with Luther and
Melanchthon with Zwingli, to seek between themselves for any possible
measure of agreement that could lead to peace. . . .

5   On the next day the four of us entered the arena in the presence of
the landgrave and a few others . . . in this and in three further
sessions . . . with witnesses, we fought our winning battle. Three times
we threw at Luther the fact that he had at other times given a different
exposition from the one he was now insisting on of those ridiculous ideas
10 of his; . . . but the dear man had nothing to say in reply — except that on
the matter of the flesh profiting nothing he said: 'You know, Zwingli,
that all the ancient writers have again and again changed their

interpretations of passages of scripture as time went on and their
judgement matured.' . . . He said: '[The bread and wine] are made into
15 the body of Christ by the utterance of these words – "This is my
body" – however great a criminal one might be who pronounces
them.' . . . These and others are examples of the countless incon-
sistencies, absurdities and follies which he babbles out like water lapping
on the shore; but we refuted him so successfully that the landgrave
20 himself has now come down on our side. . . . The landgrave himself has
given permission for our books to be read with impunity. . . .

We finally left [Marburg] with certain agreements which you will
soon see in print. The truth prevailed so manifestly that if ever anyone
was beaten it was the foolish and obstinate Luther. He was clearly
25 defeated, as any wise and fair judge would agree, although he now makes
out that he was not beaten. We have, however, achieved this much good,
that our agreement on the rest of the doctrines of the Christian religion
will prevent the papal party from hoping any longer that Luther will be
on their side.

Ulrich Zwingli, Letter to Vadian, 20 October 1529, in G. R.
Potter, *Huldrych Zwingli: Documents of Modern History*, 1978, pp
106–8

Questions

* a Who were (i) Oecolampadius and (ii) Melanchthon?
  b Why did Philip of Hesse hold the Marburg conference? What did it
  achieve and what was its greatest failure?
  c Explain the point Zwingli is making in the last sentence.
  d What criticism is Zwingli making of Luther and how far was it
  justified? Is it true to say that Luther was 'clearly defeated' (lines 24–
  5)?
* e How might Luther's view of the conference have differed from that
  of Zwingli?

8 The Peace of Augsburg, 1555

Whereas, at all the diets held during the last thirty years and more, and at
several special sessions besides, there have often been negotiations and
consultations to establish between the estates of the Holy Empire a
general, continuous and enduring peace in regard to the contending
5 religions; and several times terms of peace were drawn up, which,
however, were never sufficient for the maintenance of peace. . . .
We . . . have united and agreed with the electors, the princes and estates.

And in order that such peace, which is especially necessary in view of
the divided religions . . . may be the better established and made secure
10 and enduring between his Roman Imperial Majesty and us, on the one
hand, and the electors, princes and estates of the Holy Empire of the

German nation on the other, therefore his Imperial Majesty and we, and the electors, princes, and estates of the Holy Empire will not make war upon any estate of the empire on account of the Augsburg Confession and
15 the doctrine, religion, and faith of the same, nor injure nor do violence to those estates that hold it. . . .

On the other hand, the estates that have accepted the Augsburg Confession shall suffer his Imperial Majesty, us, and the electors, princes, and other estates of the Holy Empire, adhering to the old religion, to
20 abide in like manner by their religion, faith, church usages, ordinances, and ceremonies. . . .

But all others who are not adherents of either of the above-mentioned religions are not included in this peace, but shall be altogether excluded. . . .

25 But when our subjects and those of the electors, princes, and estates, adhering to the old religion or to the Augsburg Confession, wish, for the sake of their religion, to go with wife and children to another place in the lands, principalities, and cities of the electors, princes, and estates of the Holy Empire, and settle there, such going and coming, and the sale
30 of property and goods . . . shall be everywhere unhindered, permitted, and granted.

> J. H. Robinson, *Readings in European History*, vol II, 1906, pp 113–16

Questions

a Who was 'his Roman Imperial Majesty' (line 10)? Who issued this agreement in his name and why did the emperor not do so himself?

b Why was 'a general, continuous and enduring peace' (line 4) necessary in the Empire?

c What is meant by the 'old religion' (line 19)? What name is more usually given to those who accepted the Augsburg Confession?

* *d* Against which religious group was this agreement directed and why?

* *e* In what ways did the religious position in the Empire after 1555 differ from that in almost every other country in Europe?

VI The Reformation outside Germany

Introduction

From almost its earliest days the Lutheran movement suffered divisions; Carlstadt, for example, broke away from Luther in the 1520s. Outside Germany, there was no united protestant church either, but several different churches. Zwingli, in Zurich, set up his own version of the church and vehemently denied that he was a follower of Luther, although they had some beliefs in common.

Calvin was French-speaking, with no knowledge of German, and he developed his own ideas with a very different emphasis. In particular he was very much more authoritarian than either Luther or Zwingli and much more concerned that the church should have a predominant influence on government, local or national (extract 4). He was also much more successful than Zwingli in spreading his beliefs outside Switzerland (extract 6). Calvinism became associated with violent and long-lasting rebellion in France and the Netherlands.

Anabaptism provided a third important element in the Reformation both outside Germany and within the Empire. Because this was a very exclusive, though unorganised, set of beliefs, its members' refusal to acknowledge the authority of secular rulers meant that they were liable to be persecuted by all other churches, protestant and catholic. Anabaptism was recognised as a social problem but not as a church.

Further Reading

Owen Chadwick, *The Pelican History of the Church*, Volume III: *The Reformation* (Penguin, 1970)

A. G. Dickens, *Reformation and Society in Sixteenth-Century Europe* (Thames & Hudson, 1966)

T. H. L. Parker, *John Calvin* (Dent, 1975)

(Ed.) G. R. Potter, *Huldrych Zwingli* (Cambridge University Press, 1976)

François Wendel, *Calvin* (Fontana, 1965)

George H. Williams, *The Radical Reformation* (Westminster Press, 1962)

1 Zwingli's Statement of Belief, 1523

1 All who say that the gospel is invalid without the confirmation of the church err and slander God. . . .

xix Christ is the only mediator between God and ourselves.

xx God will give up everything in [Christ's] name, whence it follows that for our part after this life we need no mediator except him.

xxi When we pray for one another on earth, we do so in such a way that we believe that all things are to be given to us through Christ alone.

xxii Christ is our justification, from which it follows that our works, if they are of Christ, are good; but if ours, they are neither right nor good. . . .

xxiv No Christian is bound to do those things which God has not decreed; hence one may eat at all times all food. . . .

xxvii All Christian men are brethren of Christ and brothers to one another: and the title of Father should not be assumed by anyone on earth. This includes orders, sects and factions.

xxviii All that God has allowed or not forbidden is right, hence marriage is permitted to all human beings. . . .

xxxiv There is no ground in the teaching of Christ for the pretensions of the so-called spiritual authority,

xxxv Whereas the jurisdiction and authority of the secular power is based on the teachings and actions of Christ.

xxxvi All the rights and protection that the so-called spiritual authority claims belong to secular governments provided they are Christian.

xxxvii To them, likewise, all Christians owe obedience without exception,

xxxviii In so far as they do not order that which is contrary to God. . . .

xliii To sum up; that realm is best and most stable which is ruled in accordance with God's will alone, and the worst and weakest is that which is ruled arbitrarily.

From the sixty-seven theses drawn up by Zwingli for a public debate in Zurich, 29 January 1523, in G. R. Potter, *Huldrych Zwingli: Documents of Modern History*, 1978, pp 21–4

Questions

a What was the significance of clause XXIV in the development of Zwingli's career as a church reformer?

b What is meant by 'justification' as used in clause XXII (line 8)?

* c How did clauses XIX–XXII and XXVII–XXVIII differ from orthodox catholic belief?

d Summarise the argument in clauses XXXIV–XXXVIII and XLIII and explain how it affected relations between church and state in Zwingli's Zurich.

* e In which of his beliefs did Zwingli agree with Luther and which are the most obvious differences?

2 The First Treaty of Kappel, 26 June 1529

So far as the word of God is concerned no one shall be compelled to adopt
any faith. . . .

Where the mass and other ceremonies are still maintained attendance
shall not be compulsory. No preachers shall be sent, appointed or
5   provided if the majority is against them. The parishioners have freedom
of choice to accept or reject in this matter. . . .

Pensions, payments, gifts and presents from kings, princes and lords,
shall not be accepted in the future. . . . If one or more of the Five States
[Lucerne, Schwyz, Unterwalden, Uri and Zug] should enlist men in the
10   territory of the six cities [Basle, Berne, Constance, St Gall and Zurich],
take them off and send them on expeditions, both these and the lords and
masters responsible, when the facts are known, shall be punished in life
and limb. . . .

All and every decree and mandate made and issued by the six cities on
15   behalf of God's word shall stay and remain in force without hindrance or
objection truly, firmly, fixed and unchanged. Likewise where the mass,
images, church ornaments and other objects used in divine service have
been discarded, there shall be no alteration. Everyone, whatever his
allegiance, shall be left alone and shall not be induced to change by threats,
20   commands or punishment. Belief is not a matter for compulsion. . . .

Both parties shall keep their religion for so long as it suits them, and
neither side shall disturb or interfere with the other in this matter.
Further, both parties (including their spheres of influence) shall retain
their old customs and good praiseworthy usages intact as they existed
25   before these differences and hostilities without any impediment, obstacle
or prejudice.

> G. R. Potter, *Huldrych Zwingli: Documents of Modern History*,
> 1978, pp 121–2

Questions

a   What kind of 'preachers' (line 4) does the treaty refer to?

b   Which 'kings, princes or lords' might send 'pensions, payments, gifts
and presents' (line 7) and what did they want in return?

* c   In what ways was this treaty (i) similar to and (ii) different from the
Peace of Augsburg (extract 8 in section V).

* d   How successful was this treaty in solving the religious problem in
Switzerland? Why could it not be copied elsewhere?

3 The Doctrine of Predestination

The predestination by which God adopts some to the hope of life, and
adjudges others to eternal death, no man who would be thought pious
ventures simply to deny. . . . By predestination we mean the eternal
decree of God, by which he determined with himself whatever he wished

5   to happen with regard to every man. All are not created on equal terms,
but some are preordained to eternal life, others to eternal damnation; and,
accordingly, as each has been created for one or other of these ends, we say
that he has been predestinated to life or to death. This God has testified,
not only in the case of single individuals; he has also given a specimen of it
10   in the whole posterity of Abraham, to make it plain that the future
condition of each nation was entirely at his disposal. . . .

We say, then, that Scripture clearly proves this much, that God by his
eternal and immutable counsel determined once for all those whom it was
his pleasure to doom to destruction. We maintain that this counsel, as
15   regards the elect, is founded on his free mercy, without any respect to
human worth, while those whom he dooms to destruction are excluded
from access to life by a just and blameless, but at the same time
incomprehensible, judgment. In regard to the elect, we regard calling as
the evidence of election, and justification as another symbol of its
20   manifestation, until it is fully accomplished by the attainment of glory.
But as the Lord seals his elect by calling and justification, so by excluding
the reprobate either from the knowledge of his name or the sanctification
of his Spirit, he by these marks in a manner discloses the judgment which
awaits them.

John Calvin, *The Institutes of the Christian Religion*, 1536, in
L. Bernard and T. B. Hodges, *Readings in European History*, 1958,
pp 233 – 4

Questions

a   Explain what Calvin means by 'calling' and 'justification' (lines 18 –
19)

b   How did their belief that they were among the 'elect' affect the
everyday lives and behaviour of Calvinists?

* c   In what ways would (i) a Roman Catholic and (ii) a Lutheran have
disagreed with Calvin's belief as expressed in this passage?

* d   What is the importance of Calvin's book, *The Institutes of the Christian
Religion*?

4 The Authority of Civil Government

Earthly government is decreed for our life among men: it is to promote
and cherish the worship of God, to protect the sound doctrine of religion
and the position of the Church, to accommodate our lives to the society
of men, shape our behaviour in accord with civil justice, maintain
5   concord among individuals, guarantee a general peace and tranquillity. . . .

All agree that no state can be happily constituted unless its first care is to
promote piety, and that laws which, ignoring the law of God, concern
themselves with man only, are absurd . . . [therefore] Christian princes

10 and magistrates should be ashamed of their indolence if they neglect this
duty. . . .

From this follows another thing: with their minds inclined to proper
respect, subjects must prove the fact of their obedience by obeying orders,
paying taxes, undertaking public duties and burdens necessary for the
15 defence of the community, and carrying out all other commands. . . .

We are subject not only to the rule of princes who discharge their duty
to us honestly and with due trust, but also to that of all who in any way
have authority, even though nothing may be further from their minds
than a proper performance of all the duties of a prince. For though
20 the Lord testified that the magistrate is a supreme gift of His munificence . . ., He yet at the same time declares that, no matter what sort they
may be, they hold power from Him alone. Those who govern for the
common weal are true examples and specimens of His beneficence; those,
however, who lord it unjustly and despotically He has raised up to punish
25 the people's sins. . . .

The punishment of tyrants belongs to the vengeance of God, . . . we
have received no other command than to obey and be patient. . . .

However, to that obedience which I have shown to be due to the
authority of rulers there is always one exception, and that a fundamental
30 one. It must not seduce us from obedience to Him to whose will the
desires of kings must be subject.

John Calvin, *The Institutes of the Christian Religion*, 1536, in G. R.
Elton, *Renaissance and Reformation 1300—1648*, 1976, pp 216—19

Questions

  a To what extent does this extract apply to the actual circumstances of
government in Calvin's Geneva?

*   *b* Where, in the second half of the sixteenth century, did Calvinists
believe that they were being ruled 'unjustly and despotically' (line
24)? How far did they accept Calvin's advice to continue to be
obedient subjects?

*   *c* How do Calvin's views on civil government differ from those of
Philip Melanchthon (extract 5 in section V)?

*   *d* How far are the purposes of government listed in the first paragraph
of this extract still generally accepted today?

5 The Church in Geneva

[This extract is part of Calvin's reply to criticism of the church in Geneva
made by Cardinal Sadoleto in 1539.]

Although your letter has many windings, its whole purport substantially is to recover the Genevese to the power of the Roman pontiff,
5 or to what you call the faith and obedience of the Church. But, . . . you
preface with a long oration concerning the incomparable value of eternal

life. You afterward come nearer to the point, when you show that there is nothing more pestiferous to souls than a perverse worship of God; and again, that the best rule for the due worship of God is that which is preserved by the church, and that, therefore, there is no salvation for those who have violated the unity of the church unless they repent. . . .

There are three things on which the safety of the church is founded, viz., doctrine, discipline, and the sacraments, and to these a fourth is added, viz., ceremonies, by which to exercise the people in offices of piety. . . . In the sacraments, all we have attempted is to restore the native purity from which they had degenerated and so enable them to resume their dignity. Ceremonies we have in a great measure abolished, but we were compelled to do so; partly because by their multitude they had degenerated into a kind of Judaism, partly because they had filled the minds of the people with superstition, and could not possibly remain without doing the greatest injury to the piety which it was their office to promote. . . .

We loudly proclaim the communion of flesh and blood, which is exhibited to believers in the Supper; and we distinctly show that that flesh is truly meat, and that blood truly drink — that the soul, not contented with an imaginary conception, enjoys them in very truth. That presence of Christ, by which we are ingrafted in Him, we by no means exclude from the Supper, nor shroud in darkness, though we hold that there must be no local limitation, that the glorious body of Christ must not be degraded to earthly elements; that there must be no fiction of transubstantiating the bread into Christ, and afterward worshipping it as Christ.

John Calvin, *Epistle to Sadoleto*, 1539, in H. J. Hillerbrand, *The Protestant Reformation*, 1968, pp 154, 159–60, 165

Questions

a What is meant by (i) 'the Roman pontiff' (line 4) and (ii) 'transubstantiating the bread into Christ' (lines 30–31)?

b What was Calvin's belief about the presence of Christ at the Lord's Supper, as explained in this passage?

* c How had Geneva 'violated the unity of the Church' (line 11)? How would Calvin have justified this 'violation'?

* d Why did Calvin say 'ceremonies we have in a great measure abolished' (line 17)? How did a Calvinist service differ from the Mass?

e By 'discipline', Calvin meant church supervision of its members' behaviour. How was this supervision exercised and with what aspects of moral and social behaviour was it particularly concerned?

6 The Triumph of Protestantism in Scotland

Our Confession was publicly read . . . in audience of the whole

Parliament; where were present, not only such as professed Christ Jesus, but also a great number of the adversaries of our religion, . . . who were commanded in God's name to object, if they could, any thing against that doctrine. Some of our Ministers were present, standing upon their feet, ready to have answered, in case any would have defended the Papistry, and impugned our affirmatives: but while that no objection was made, there was a day appointed to voting in that and other heads. Our Confession was read, every article by itself, over again, as they were written in order, and the votes of every man were required accordingly. Of the Temporal Estate, only voted in the contrary the Earl of Atholl, the Lords Somerville and Borthwick; and yet for their dissenting they produced no better reason, but, 'We will believe as our fathers believed.' The Bishops (papistical, we mean) spake nothing. The rest of the whole three Estates by their public votes affirmed the doctrine; and many, the rather, would nor durst say nothing in the contrary; for this was the vote of the Earl Marischal — 'It is long since I have had some favour unto the truth, and since that I have had a suspicion of the Papistical religion; but, I praise my God, this day has fully resolved me in the one and the other.' . . .

After the voting and ratification of this our Confession by the whole body of the Parliament, there were also pronounced two Acts, the one against the Mass and the abuse of the Sacrament, and the other against the Supremacy of the Pope.

> John Knox, *History of the Reformation in Scotland*, 1584, in G. R. Elton, *Renaissance and Reformation 1300–1648*, 1976, pp 222–3

Questions

a   What is meant by the 'Temporal Estate' (line 11)? What were the 'three Estates' (line 15)?

b   'Our Confession' (line 1) was a statement of the beliefs of the reformed church. What were its main terms?

* c   Why was there so little opposition to the Reformation in Scotland?
* d   How far does John Knox deserve the credit for its introduction?
* e   From the evidence in this extract, how does the way in which the Reformation was introduced in Scotland compare with that in other countries?

7   Accusations against an Anabaptist and his Defence

1 That he and his fellows have acted against the imperial command.

2 He taught, held and believed that the body and blood of Christ are not in the sacrament.

3 He taught and believed that infant baptism does not help to salvation. . . .

6 He said that one should take no oath to obey authority. . . .

9 He said: If the Turk came, he should not be resisted, and if war were justified he would rather fight against Christians than against Turks. . . .

10 Then [the accused] spoke and answered without fear.

To the first: that we have acted against the imperial command we do not admit; for that says that one should not adhere to Luther's doctrine and delusion but only to the gospel and Word of God; and so have we done. . . .

15 To the second: that the sacrament does not contain the real body of our Lord Jesus Christ, that we admit; for the Scripture says thus: Christ ascended into heaven and sits on the right hand of his heavenly father where he will judge the quick and the dead. It follows that if he be in heaven and not in the bread, he cannot be eaten corporeally.

20 To the third: concerning baptism we say: infant baptism is not useful for salvation. . . . Also he who believes and is baptised shall be saved. . . .

To the sixth: we hold that we are not to take an oath to the authorities, for the Lord says 'Swear not at all . . . but let your communication be Yea, Yea, Nay, Nay.' . . .

25 To the ninth: if the Turk comes he shall not be resisted, for it is written, Thou shalt not kill. We are not to defend ourselves against the Turk and other persecutors, but are to pray heartily to God that He be our protection and defence. . . . The Turk is a true Turk and knows nothing of the Christian faith; he is a Turk in the flesh. So you would be Christians

30 and boast of Christ but persecute Christ's true witnesses and are Turks in the spirit.

G. R. Elton, *Renaissance and Reformation 1300—1648*, 1976, pp 197—8

Questions

a   Explain the views of the accused with regard to (i) the sacrament and (ii) baptism.

*
b   How did his attitude to the sacrament differ from that of (i) Roman Catholics and (ii) other protestants?

c   How successful do you think his defence against the first accusation would be?

*
d   What is there in the defence to explain the intense hostility felt by almost all other Christians to the Anabaptists? What other reasons were there for this antagonism?

VII   The Counter-Reformation

Introduction

Was the Counter-Reformation a reaction to the protestant Reformation or was it part of the same reforming movement? The answer to this question depends to a considerable extent on one's own religious position, some protestants favouring the first interpretation and Roman Catholics the second (extract 1). Certainly the work of the Council of Trent was largely defensive, strengthening the church by redefining its doctrine and improving its discipline, but this was in preparation for an offensive against the protestants and one which had a considerable measure of success.

The agents of the Counter-Reformation, including new or reformed religious orders such as the Capuchins and especially the Society of Jesus (extract 2), made it possible for the Tridentine reforms to be put into effect in many areas and they also tried to spread their faith to other parts of the world, including America and the Far East (extract 5 in section II). Even so, it was many years before the reforms were fully enforced throughout the catholic world because of the reluctance of kings, princes and cardinals to accept and implement them (extracts 5 and 6), if this meant in any way limiting their own privileges and prerogatives.

Further Reading

A. G. Dickens, *The Counter-Reformation* (Thames & Hudson, 1969)
Pierre Janelle, *The Catholic Reformation* (Collier-Macmillan, 1971)
G. W. Searle, *The Counter-Reformation* (University of London Press, 1974)

1   The Catholic Reformation

While an amendment of Church conditions was possible without an evangelical revival, that revival must consist mostly in chastening the spirit of the times, must be a combination of a cultured Christianity and a christianized Renaissance. This combination, which was to be the essence of the Catholic Reformation, had its root as early as the late fifteenth century in the movement known as Christian humanism. It was the natural reaction of the genuine piety of the body of the Church against corruption in its head. Its progress was to be simultaneous with the progress of the reforming party; its representatives were slowly to force their way into the College of Cardinals, the curial offices, and eventually to conquer the papacy itself; and it was then that their efforts were to mature and bear fruit in the Council of Trent, while they also inspired the work of the Society of Jesus. . . .

The Christian humanists ardently wished for a religious revival. They aimed at a true reformation – not merely a correction of abuses, but a cleansing and a lifting up of hearts, grounded on . . . a deeper love of Christ. They did not want every man to set up as a theologian; but they wanted him to read the Bible humbly and piously, and to gather from it spiritual truths. They insisted on the importance of preaching . . . in words that all might grasp, that might win through love rather than strike with fear. In this respect they were decidedly different from the early Protestants, both in Germany and England. . . .

The state of Christianity was improving; and it would have improved much faster, and wholly forestalled the Protestant upheaval, had the papacy been free to concentrate upon home problems. Unfortunately, the correction of abuses, even indeed, some years later, the suppression of the German revolt, ranked only second among the difficulties which Rome had to contend with. Just about the year 1517 the whole of Christendom was threatened with a Turkish invasion, . . . while the ambition of various Christian princes constantly endangered the independence of the Holy See.

Pierre Janelle, *The Catholic Reformation*, 1971, pp 28–9, 32

Questions

a   Explain the phrases the 'reaction of the genuine piety of the body of the Church against corruption in its head' (lines 7–8) and 'a true reformation' (line 15).

b   How, according to the author, did the 'reforming party' (line 9) achieve its ends?

*   c   How did the preaching of 'the early Protestants' (lines 21–2) differ from the catholic ideal?

*   d   Do you agree with the author that 'the Protestant upheaval' (line 24) might have been forestalled?

e   How did the 'ambition of various Christian princes' (line 30) endanger the independence of the Holy See?

*   f   How do the approach and attitude of the author, a Roman Catholic, differ from those to be expected of a protestant historian?

2   The Establishment of the Society of Jesus

He who desires to fight for God under the banner of the cross in our

society — which we wish to distinguish by the name of Jesus, — and to serve God alone and the Roman pontiff, his vicar on earth, after a solemn vow of perpetual chastity, shall set this thought before his mind, that he is
5 a part of a society founded for the especial purpose of providing for the advancement of souls in Christian life and doctrine and for the propagation of the faith through public preaching and the ministry of the word of God, spiritual exercises and deeds of charity, and in particular through the training of the young and ignorant in Christianity and
10 through the spiritual consolation of the faithful in Christ in hearing confessions; and he shall take care to keep first God and next the purpose of this organisation always before his eyes. . . .

All the members shall realise, and shall recall daily, as long as they live, that this society as a whole and in every part is fighting for God under
15 faithful obedience to one most holy lord, the pope, and to the other Roman pontiffs who succeed him. And . . . we have adjudged that . . . we should each be bound by a peculiar vow, in addition to the general obligation, that whatever the present Roman pontiff, or any future one, may from time to time decree regarding the welfare of souls and the
20 propagation of the faith, we are pledged to obey without evasion or excuse, instantly, so far as in us lies, whether he send us to the Turks or any other infidels, even to those who inhabit the regions men call the Indies; whether to heretics or schismatics, or, on the other hand, to certain of the faithful. . . .
25 Subordinates shall, indeed, both for the sake of the wide activities and also for the assiduous practice, never sufficiently to be commended, of humility, be bound always to obey the commander in every matter pertaining to the organisation of the society.

From the papal bull of 1540, establishing the Society of Jesus, in J. H. Robinson, *Readings in European History*, vol II, 1906, pp 162–3

Questions

a Who was 'the Roman pontiff' (line 3) at this time?
b To which groups of people does the phrase 'heretics or schismatics' (line 23) probably refer?
c What was the significance of 'spiritual exercises' (line 8)?
* d Who established the Society of Jesus? In what ways did it (i) resemble and (ii) differ from the traditional monastic orders?
* e What part was played by the Society in the work of the Counter-Reformation? How successful was it?

3 The Need for Reform

Most reverend Fathers, As the matters to be dealt with in this sacred congress for God's glory and the Church's good increased, we who bore the office of presidents and legates of the Apostolic See thought it our bounden duty often to use words of exhortation or of warning. Nor must we change our way in this second session. . . .

When we exhort you to do what befits so great a gathering or, on the contrary, warn you, we are exhorting or warning ourselves, who are in the same bark with you, and are exposed with you to the same dangers and the same storms. . . .

Therefore, that we may begin as we should, all be warned in this beginning: each of us should above all things keep before his eyes the things that are expected of this holy council. Each one will easily see therein what is the duty resting upon him. To put it briefly, these duties are what are contained in the bull summoning the council, viz., the uprooting of heresies, the reformation of ecclesiastical discipline and of morals, and lastly the external peace of the whole Church. These are the things we must see to, or rather for which we must untiringly pray in order that by God's mercy they may be done. . . .

Therefore what, in His great love of God the Father and in His mercifulness towards our race, Christ did, justice now enacts of us that we should do. Before the tribunal of God's mercy we, the shepherds, should make ourselves responsible for all the evils now burdening the flock of Christ. The sins of all we should take upon ourselves, not in generosity but in justice; because the truth is that of these evils we are in great part the cause, and therefore we should implore the divine mercy through Jesus Christ.

> Cardinal Reginald Pole, *An Appeal to the Council of Trent*, 1546, in J. B. Ross and M. M. McLaughlin, *The Portable Renaissance Reader*, 1977, pp 665–8

Questions

a What were 'legates' (line 3) and 'the bull' (line 14)?

b Why did 'ecclesiastical discipline and . . . morals' (lines 15–16) need reforming?

c What does Pole mean by the Council's duty with regard to 'the external peace of the whole Church' (line 16)?

d In what sense was it true that priests were 'in great part the cause' of 'the sins of all' (lines 23–5)?

e How did it happen that an Englishman was one of the presidents of the Council of Trent?

4 Some Decrees of the Council of Trent

If anyone says that the New Testament does not provide for a distinct, visible priesthood; or that this priesthood has not any power of consecrating and offering up the true body and blood of the Lord, and of forgiving and retaining sins, but is only an office and bare ministry of

5   preaching the gospel; or that those who do not preach are not priests at all;
      let him be anathema. . . .
          If anyone says that in the Catholic Church there is not a hierarchy
      instituted by divine ordination, consisting of bishops, priests and
      ministers; let him be anathema.
10   If anyone says that the sacraments of the new law were not all instituted
      by Jesus Christ, our Lord; or that they are more or less than seven, to wit,
      baptism, confirmation, the eucharist, penance, extreme unction, orders,
      and matrimony; or even that any one of these seven is not truly and
      properly a sacrament; let him be anathema. . . .
15   In order that the faithful may approach and receive the sacraments with
      greater reverence and devotion of mind, this holy Council enjoins on all
      bishops that, not only when they are themselves about to administer them
      to the people, they shall first explain, in a manner suited to the capacity of
      those who receive them, the efficacy and use of those sacraments, but they
20   shall endeavour that the same be done piously and prudently by every
      parish priest; and this even in the vernacular tongue, if need be, and if it
      can conveniently be done. . . .
          This holy Council, being minded that these things are of the greatest
      importance towards restoring ecclesiastical discipline, admonishes all
25   bishops that, often meditating thereon, they show themselves conform-
      able to their office by their actual deeds and the actions of their lives,
      which is a kind of perpetual sermon; but, above all, that they so order
      their whole conversation that others may thence be able to derive
      examples of frugality, modesty, continency, and of that holy humility
30   which so much commends us to God.
          J. H. Robinson, *Readings in European History*, vol II, 1906, pp
          159–60

Questions

*   a   What name is usually given to the doctrine concerning 'the true body
          and blood of the Lord' (line 3)? Why did this doctrine cause so much
          trouble in the sixteenth century?
      b   Explain what is meant by 'anathema' (line 6), 'extreme unction' (line
          12), and 'orders' (line 12)?
      c   Which aspects of the doctrines in the second and third paragraphs
          were rejected by all protestants?
      d   What criticisms of early sixteenth-century bishops are implicit in the
          last two paragraphs of this extract?
*   e   Who first summoned the Council of Trent and why did it seem
          necessary to hold such a council?
*   f   How far were the Tridentine decrees successful in raising standards
          among catholic clergy and bishops by the end of the sixteenth
          century?

5 Princes and the Reform of the Roman Catholic Church

The Council of Trent opened after an infinity of delays upon 13
December 1545, with only twenty-eight bishops present. The Emperor
and the Pope wanted the Council to perform different functions. The
Emperor hankered for religious peace in Germany, by reforming the
5   abuses and corruptions of the Church and by giving to the Lutherans
certain concessions, like the marriage of the clergy and communion in
both kinds. He therefore desired the Council to attend to the questions of
discipline and leave the questions of doctrine, which his experience of
divines led him to think insoluble. The Pope on the contrary instructed
10   his legates, who presided, that the Council must first treat the questions of
doctrine. It was therefore agreed that doctrine and discipline should be
treated in parallel. But of the three sessions during which the Council sat
the first was chiefly concerned with the doctrinal definitions believed
needful upon the questions in controversy with the Protestants, and the
15   last was chiefly concerned with those efforts at disciplinary regulation and
correction which the traditionalists meant when they used the word
reform. . . .

In the Protestant countries the reform was often carried through by the
princes against the Pope. In the Catholic countries the process was not so
20   different — it was carried through by the ecclesiastics with the active or
reluctant assistance of the princes. In Catholic France and parts of south
Germany the decrees could not even be received, and Spain helped itself
to what it preferred. It was not easy to reform the episcopate when so
many Catholic kings, including those of France and Spain, exercised an
25   almost absolute control over the choice of men to be bishops. As late as
June 1569, the Venetian ambassador in Paris said that at the French court
'they deal in bishoprics and abbeys as merchants trade in pepper and
cinnamon.' The Council of Trent was an effective reforming council in
Italy; elsewhere it was an encouragement and stimulus to reform.

Owen Chadwick, *The Reformation*, 1964, pp 274, 280

Questions

* a   What experience had the emperor had which made him think that
       questions of doctrine were 'insoluble' (line 9)?
   b   Why was the pope not able to agree with the emperor over this
       question?
   c   What is meant by 'communion in both kinds' (lines 6—7) and
       'questions of discipline' (lines 7—8)?
* d   In what ways was the church in Italy reformed?
* e   Why were many catholic rulers not anxious to introduce the decrees
       of the Council of Trent? Why, in the end, did they do so?

6   Did the College of Cardinals Change?

The contrast between the worldly, luxurious and unruly cardinalate of the Renaissance and the reformed, more ascetic, ecclesiastically-minded and submissive cardinalate of the Counter-Reformation is one that has become well established in sixteenth-century historiography. . . .

5   Overall, can one assume that the cardinals of the Counter-Reformation lived in less luxurious style and on more slender revenues than those of the High Renaissance? . . .

The style of life of even the cardinals with some reputation for austerity and saintliness could be lavish. The Venetian envoy estimated the annual
10   revenue of Carlo Borromeo at 52,000 *scudi*, though largely spent on charities, dowries on poor girls, or paying the debts of his brother. 'He only harbours 150 persons in his palace many of whom are obliged to defray their expenses, and to live in the Roman fashion, that is, on hope. The Jesuits have induced him, besides his own natural inclination, to lead
15   the holy life which he does. The Pope, who would have liked to see him livelier and spend more, has often exhorted him to lead a less austere existence; but he has not changed his ways.' Perhaps equally symbolic of the cross-currents of the Counter-Reformation is the sumptuous tomb in which Carlo Borromeo lies buried in the cathedral of Milan.
20   The period under review saw a tension between certain new ideals and aspirations concerning the ecclesiastical life and traditional notions of rank and hierarchy. Traditionally, and this one may argue remained the stronger attitude, magnificence and rank were closely associated in the minds of contemporaries. A certain style of life was expected from a
25   cardinal and equally the magnanimity, hospitality, patronage and charity which wealth made possible.

A. V. Antonovics, *Counter-Reformation Cardinals: 1534−90*, European Studies Review, 1972, pp 301, 322−3

Questions

a   What were the chief faults of the cardinals before the Counter-Reformation?
*
b   Why was Carlo Borromeo so important an influence in the Counter-Reformation church? Why should the Jesuits have sought to influence him and other cardinals?
c   Why was it so difficult for the cardinals of the second half of the sixteenth century to live less luxuriously than their predecessors?
*
d   Which of the decrees of the Council of Trent particularly affected cardinals and their life-style?
*
e   How much change was there in the cardinalate between 1530 and 1580?

VIII   Philip II of Spain

Introduction

Philip II ruled as much land as his father had done, but his empire, especially after the acquisition of Portugal and her colonies, was much more Iberian. Philip himself was essentially a Spaniard and never left the peninsula after 1559.

The first part of his reign was relatively peaceful and successful, with the climax apparently marked by success in the battle of Lepanto in 1571, though the importance of this battle has been challenged (extract 7 in section XI). At about the same time there was increasing trouble in the Netherlands (section IX) and when William of Orange was outlawed in 1580 he reacted by publishing his *Apologia*. This is the origin of the 'Black Legend' about Philip II and, to those already receptive to this kind of propaganda, it seemed certain proof of Philip's wickedness (extract 3).

Philip saw himself as the 'champion of the Roman Catholic church' and devoted much of his effort in foreign policy to defending and strengthening the church, although this does not mean that he was always in sympathy or agreement with the aims of the papacy, and there is little evidence that he was prepared to sacrifice the interests of Spain for the good of the church.

The defeat of the Armada can be regarded as a turning-point because, until 1588, most of his policies had been successful, whereas during Philip's last years, events in the Netherlands, England and France tended to go against Spain. Philip must have realised that things were not going well, but this is not apparent in his advice to his son (extract 4). Spain was suffering from inflation, high taxation and economic depression, even if it was not yet recognised that this marked a decline from some recent 'golden age' (extract 7).

Further Reading

Fernand Braudel, *The Mediterranean and the Mediterranean World in the Age of Philip II* (Collins, 1972)

Edward Grierson, *King of Two Worlds: Philip II of Spain* (Collins, 1974)

Henry Kamen, *The Spanish Inquisition* (New English Library, 1977)

Garrett Mattingly, *The Defeat of the Spanish Armada* (Cape, 1959)

Geoffrey Parker, *Philip II* (Hutchinson, 1979)

Peter Pierson, *Philip II of Spain* (Thames & Hudson, 1975)

1 Advice from Charles V

I think I need not endeavour to exhort you to imitate the conduct which I
have adhered to during the course of my life, nearly all of which I have
passed in difficult enterprises and laborious employment, in the defence of
the empire, in propagating the holy faith of Jesus Christ, and in
5 preserving my peoples in peace and security. I will only say that at the
beginning of your reign the two advantages you have – of being my son
and of looking like me – will, if I am not mistaken, win for you the love
of your subjects. . . .

The charge of ruling the realms which today I place upon your
10 shoulders is more trying than the government of Spain which is a
kingdom of ancient inheritance, firm and assured; whereas the acquisition
of the states of Flanders, Italy, and the other provinces into whose
possession you are to enter, is more recent, and they are exposed to more
difficulties and upheavals, especially because they have for neighbours
15 powerful and belligerent princes. . . .

A prince must preserve his credit with the merchants, which he will
easily achieve if he takes precise care to pay them both their capital and the
interest arising on it. . . .

And since it is impossible for princes (especially those possessing several
20 realms) to govern all alone, they must be assisted by ministers who will
help them to carry so heavy a burden. . . .

The three principal qualities called for in a minister are sound sense,
love of his prince, and uprightness. Sound sense makes them capable of
administration; love ensures that they have their master's interests at
25 heart; and uprightness helps them to discharge their business ef-
ficiently. . . . But while it is difficult to find such men . . . experience
shows that all princes who have had this advantage have ruled their
peoples with glory and success. . . . That prince may be called very
unfortunate who has neither the ability to rule by himself nor the good
30 sense to follow wise counsels. . . . Do not think that any prince, however
wise and able he may be, can do without good ministers.

Charles V, *Instructions to Philip II, His Son*, 1555, in G. R. Elton,
Renaissance and Reformation 1300–1648, 1970, pp 136–8

Questions

a   In what ways had Charles V defended his empire and propagated
Christianity?

b   What experience had Charles of the 'powerful and belligerent' neighbours (lines 14–15) of Italy and Flanders?

* c   How far did Philip II follow his father's advice in relation to (i) 'credit
with the merchants' (line 16) and (ii) assistance from ministers? Was
he as good as his father at choosing ministers?

* d   How far were Philip II's difficulties due to his failure to follow his
father's advice? What other causes were there for his problems?

2 A Contemporary Estimate of Philip II

The Catholic king was born in Spain . . . and spent a great part of his youth in that kingdom. Here, in accordance with the customs of the country and the wishes of his father and mother . . . he was treated with all the deference and respect which seemed due to the son of the greatest
5   emperor whom Christendom had ever had, and to the heir to such a number of realms and to such grandeur. . . .

Although the king resembles his father in his face and speech, in his attention to his religious duties, and in his habitual kindness and good faith, he nevertheless differs from him in several of those respects in which
10 the greatness of rulers, after all, lies. The emperor was addicted to war, which he well understood; the king knows but little of it and has no love for it. The emperor undertook great enterprises with enthusiasm; his son avoids them. The father was fond of planning great things and would in the end realise his wishes by his skill; his son, on the contrary, pays less
15 attention to augmenting his own greatness than to hindering that of others. . . . The father was guided in all matters by his own opinion; the son follows the opinion of others.

In the king's eyes no nation is superior to the Spaniards. It is among them that he lives, it is they that he consults, and it is they that direct his
20 policy; in all this he is acting quite contrary to the habit of his father. He thinks little of the Italians and Flemish and still less of the Germans. Although he may employ the chief men of all the countries over which he rules, he admits none of them to his secret counsels, but utilizes their services only in military matters, and then perhaps not so much because
25 he really esteems them, as in the hope that he will in this way prevent his enemies from making use of them.

> Report of Michele Suriano, the Venetian ambassador in Spain, 1559, in J. H. Robinson, *Readings in European History*, vol II, 1906, pp 168–9

Questions

a Do you think that Philip's education was responsible for his attitude to his non-Spanish subjects?

b What evidence is there to support the criticism of Philip in the last sentence of this extract? Do you think that this increased his difficulties with the Netherlands and other parts of his empire?

c At the beginning of his reign it may have been true to say that Philip avoided 'great enterprises' (line 12), but was it true of his entire reign?

d Was Philip more concerned to hinder the greatness of others than to augment his own?

e Is the ambassador's generally critical report fair to Philip?

3 An Attack on Philip II

[Philip II] seems not to have remembered the common maxim, that whoever ventures to accuse another, ought to be well assured that he himself is innocent. And yet is not this king, who has endeavoured to stigmatise my lawful marriage with infamy, the husband of his own
5   niece? It will be said by his partisans, that he previously obtained a dispensation from the pope. But does not the voice of nature cry aloud against such an incestuous conjunction? And in order to make room for this marriage, is it not true that he put to death his former wife, the mother of his children, the daughter and sister of kings of France?
10   It was not a single murder that was perpetrated for the sake of this extraordinary marriage. His son, too, his only son was sacrificed, in order to furnish the pope with a pretext for so unusual a dispensation; which was granted, in order to prevent the Spanish monarchy from being left without a male heir. This was the true cause of the death of Don Carlos,
15   against whom some misdemeanours were alleged; but not a single crime sufficient to justify his condemnation, much less to vindicate a father for imbruing his hands in the blood of his son. . . .
It is against me chiefly that his designs are directed. 'Were I removed,' he says, 'either by death or banishment, tranquillity would be restored.'
20   You will easily conceive what tranquillity he means if you call to mind your condition, before I returned into the Netherlands, when you groaned under the tyranny of the Duke of Alva. Would to heaven that by my banishment or death you could be delivered from your calamities! . . . I leave it to you, to whom alone it belongs, to determine,
25   whether my life and presence be repugnant or conducive to the interest of the provinces. To you only, and not to the King of Spain, I am accountable for my conduct.

> William of Orange, *Apologia*, 1580, in J. C. Rule and J. J. TePaske, *The Character of Philip II: The Problem of Moral Judgments in History*, 1966, pp 8 – 10

Questions

a Who were the two wives referred to, 'his own niece' (lines 4 – 5) and 'the daughter and sister of kings of France' (line 9)? What happened to them?

b What actually happened to Don Carlos? Why was his death generally regarded as having taken place in suspicious circumstances?

c What basis was there in fact for the accusations made in the first two paragraphs?

d Why should the Duke of Alva's rule of the Netherlands be described as 'tyranny' (line 22)? Can this description be justified by the duke's policies?

* *e* Give reasons why William's 'life and presence' were either 'repugnant' or 'conducive' to the interest of the Netherlands (lines 25 – 6).

4   Instructions to His Son, Philip III

Strive, my son, to love God with all your heart, for no one can be saved who does not love Him. . . .

If in your mind you contemplate doing something of importance, consult your confessor, or some wise man with high moral principles, in
5 order to determine the most suitable course to follow. Let those who become your friends and confidants be good, vertuous, and respected men, whether they be laymen or clerics. . . .

You should take pride in according your subjects peace and justice; assure this particularly for priests and clergymen, that discord and
10 injustice do not disturb them and their prayers to God for you and your kingdom; strive that they do not lack justice. . . . Do not wage war, especially against Christians, without great forethought and just cause; and if it is necessary to do so, let it be without harm to churches and innocent persons. If you are at war with another, whenever it is within
15 your power, strive for peace; and if you are not directly involved, mediate between those at war in order that discord cease.

See to it that ministers of justice, councilmen, chief magistrates, and judges be vertuous and wise; and secretly inform yourself as to the administration of their offices. Always be obedient to the Roman Church
20 and Supreme Pontiff, having him for your spiritual father. The expenses of your court should be moderate and conform to reason.

> Philip II, dictated shortly before his death, 1598, in J. C. Rule and J. J. TePaske, *The Character of Philip II: The Problem of Moral Judgments in History*, 1966, pp 6–7

Questions

a   Were Philip II's wars always for a 'just cause' (line 12)? What subject was most often a cause of these wars?

*
b   In what ways had Philip followed the outlines of policy he recommended to his son?

*
*
c   In what ways had he most obviously deviated from them?

d   In what ways does this extract seem typical of Philip II? How does it differ from the advice which Philip himself had received from his own father (extract 1)?

5   The Spanish Inquisition

In 1563 the Council of Trent closed its final session, and with this the Catholic Counter-Reformation reached a position of no compromise in the European struggle. Catholic Europe, and with it Catholic Spain, turned to the attack.
5   How far had the Inquisition served to protect Spain from the inroads of foreign contagion? It had certainly allowed the old orthodoxy to maintain its Reconquest mentality and racialist views. A recent Spanish

study on the Inquisition affirms clearly and unequivocally that illuminism
and even Lutheranism owed their Spanish origins to *conversos*, and that
10 these doctrines were therefore aberrations produced by non-Spanish
minorities. This implies that the Inquisition was defending the purity of
the Spanish race. Yet this was precisely the argument used in the sixteenth
century by antisemites. As archbishop Siliceo of Toledo claimed in
1547:

15   It is said, and it is considered true, that the principal heretics of Germany, who
        have destroyed all that nation and have introduced great heresies, are
        descendants of Jews.

The opinion was common in Spain. Thus the struggle against Luther in
1559 was just a continuation of the struggle against the Jews in 1480. One
20 crusade overlapped another. So did fact and fancy. There is no doubt that
converso heterodoxy played an important part in the religious problems of
Spain. . . . Eminent Erasmists like Vergara were of *converso* origin, and
so were others suspected of Lutheranism. . . . But the systematic
identification of *conversos* with the principal heresies of the day could not
25 possibly be substantiated. That it was seriously believed at the time is
proof that the Inquisition, essentially an instrument of the ruling class,
was still seen to be performing an important function in preserving the
religious and racial unity of Spain.
                Henry Kamen, *The Spanish Inquisition*, 1965, pp 88–9

Questions

a   Who were the *conversos* (line 9)? Why were they so unpopular with
    most people in Spain?
b   What was the 'Reconquest' (line 7)? Explain the sentence which refers
    to it.
*   c   Why was it important, in the sixteenth century, that the Inquisition
    should preserve 'the religious and racial unity of Spain' (line 28)? Does
    this explain why most people approved of the activities of the
    Inquisition?
*   d   What aspects of the Inquisition and its procedures have given it such a
    bad reputation outside Spain since the sixteenth century? How far did
    it deserve such a reputation?

6   Reaction to Disaster

Philip had no opportunity to display his famous constancy in the face of
unexpected disaster, because the full extent of the defeat [of the Armada]
was broken to him by slow degrees. Some time before the duke reached
Santander, Philip had read Medina Sidonia's letter of August 21st with its
5   accompanying *Diario* and listened to Captain Balthazar de Zuñiga's
depressing report. He had heard both Parma's account of the missed
rendezvous and, later, rumours of wrecks on the Irish coast. Nor is it

believable that Philip would . . . have blamed the winds and waves of
the God his fleet had sailed to serve, especially since he had learnt from
Medina Sidonia's *Diario* that, up to August 21st, at least, the Armada had
had all the best of it in the way of weather.

That Philip faced the bad news, as it came in, with dignity and
constancy one can well believe, though there are limits to the constancy
that can be expected of any human frame. He was seriously ill that
autumn — an illness in the opinion of the diplomatic corps brought on, or
at least aggravated, by anxiety and disappointment. . . .

But if Philip felt the blow of Fate, and showed that he felt it, he was not
crushed by it. Almost as soon as he learned the extent of his losses he was
assuring ambassadors that he would build another fleet stronger than the
last, if he had to melt down every piece of plate on his table and every
silver candlestick in the Escurial. It did not quite come to that, but
American bullion had to be supplemented by scraping the cupboards of
Castile and striking new bargains with Genoese bankers.

Garrett Mattingly, *The Defeat of the Spanish Armada*, 1959, pp
326—7

Questions

a Who were Parma and Medina Sidonia? What part had each played in
the 'enterprise of England'?

b What was the Escurial?

c How important had 'the winds and waves' (line 8) been in the defeat
of the Armada?

*

d What success did the later Armadas have?

*

e Can it be argued that the Armada's defeat marked a turning-point in
Philip's reign?

7 Did Spain Decline?

The point is not that Spain did not suffer crises and reverses, for the
contrary is obviously true. The real questions are: did those reverses
represent the collapse of a once highly flourishing society? Were the
reverses so extensive as to cover nearly two centuries, and so universal as
to embrace all aspects of activity? The answer in both cases is a firmly
negative one that must throw serious doubt on the relevance of 'decline'.
The main consideration to bear in mind is that Spain had never been an
economically strong nation. . . . By the end of the reign of Charles v the
economy had made no significant strides forward, yet already the
historians invite us to consider the country as being set for decline. It is
difficult to see how so undeveloped a nation could have 'declined' before
ever becoming rich. One solution to the difficulty is that Spain had indeed
flourished, but that was in the time of the Catholic Monarchs. . . .

The wool trade . . . reached its height in the early sixteenth century,

15 stimulating financial activity in northern Castile. . . . Wool was dominated by the foreign markets in Flanders, Italy and France. . . . Spain
never broke away from this system. Domination by foreign capital,
which was implicit in the resulting unfavourable terms of trade, led to an
invasion of the vulnerable home market by foreign goods. . . . The wool
20 which was one of the bulwarks both of the peasant and the government,
and formed a key sector of the economy, became the means to bind
Spanish interests to foreign manufactures. . . .

The riches of America opened up another, overlapping system of
dependence, when bullion poured into Andalusia and northern Castile.
25 What happened is well known. Rapid wealth came to the underde-
veloped metropolis, which however proved unable to make up the
balance of trade with its own produce. . . . The foreign markets and their
agents now extended their operations to America, so that Spain in its
relations with the New World found itself acting largely as an entrepot
30 for foreign goods.

> Henry Kamen, *The Decline of Spain: A Historical Myth?*, Past and
> Present no. 81, 1978, pp 35, 41−3

Questions

a Who were 'the Catholic Monarchs' (line 13)? What were their most
   important achievements?
b Why were the terms of trade 'unfavourable' (line 18) to Spain in the
   first part of the sixteenth century?
c Which 'foreign markets and their agents' (lines 27−8) were most
   concerned with both the wool trade and the financial business which
   resulted from the import of bullion?
* d What is usually meant by 'the decline of Spain'?
* e Why does the author believe that this concept is wrong?

8 Philip ii: A Summary

The fundamental characteristic of Philip ii's empire was its Spanishness —
or rather Castilianism — a fact which did not escape the contemporaries
of the Prudent King, whether friend or foe; they saw him as a spider sitting
motionless at the centre of the web. But if Philip, after returning from
5 Flanders in September, 1559, never again left the Peninsula, was it simply
from inclination, from a pronounced personal preference for things
Spanish? Or might it not also have been largely dictated by necessity? We
have seen how the states of Charles v, one after another, silently refused to
support the expense of his campaigns. Their deficits made Sicily, Naples,
10 Milan and later the Netherlands, burdens on the empire, dependent places
where it was no longer possible for the Emperor to reside. Philip ii had
had personal experience of this in the Netherlands where, during his stay
between 1555 and 1559, he had relied exclusively on money imported

from Spain or on the hope of its arrival. And it was now becoming difficult for the ruler to obtain such assistance without being in person close to its original source. Philip II's withdrawal to Spain was a tactical withdrawal towards American silver. . . .

That the centre of the web lay in Spain bred many consequences; in the first place the growing, blind affection of the mass of Spanish people for the king who had chosen to live among them. Philip II was as much beloved of the people of Castile as his father had been by the good folk of the Low Countries. A further consequence was the logical predominance of Peninsular appointments, interests and prejudices during Philip's reign: of those harsh haughty men, the intransigent nobles of Castile whom Philip employed on foreign missions, while for the conduct of everyday affairs and bureaucratic routine he showed a marked preference for commoners. . . . Philip II's refusal to move encouraged the growth of a sedentary administration whose bags need no longer be kept light for travelling. The weight of paper became greater than ever. The other parts of the empire slipped imperceptibly into the role of satellites and Castile into that of the metropolitan power. . . .

That Philip II was not fully aware of these changes, that he considered himself to be continuing the policy initiated by Charles V, his father's disciple as well as successor, is certainly true. . . .

But circumstances were to dictate radical changes. Only the trappings of empire survived. The grandiose ambitions of Charles V were doomed by the beginning of Philip's reign, even before the treaty of 1559, and brutally liquidated by the financial disaster of 1557. The machinery of empire had to be overhauled and repaired before it could be started again. Charles V had never in his headlong career been forced to brake so sharply: the drastic return to peace in the early days of Philip's reign was the sign of latter-day weakness. Grand designs were not revived until later and then less as the result of the personal desires of the sovereign than through force of circumstance. . . .

After the 1580s, shipments of bullion from the New World reached an unprecedented volume. The time was now ripe for Granvelle to return to the Spanish court. But it would be wrong to think that the imperialism which appeared at the end of the reign was solely the result of his presence. The great war which began in the 1580s was fundamentally a struggle for control of the Atlantic Ocean, the new centre of gravity of the world. Its outcome would decide whether the Atlantic was in future to be ruled by Catholics or Protestants, northerners or Iberians, for the Atlantic was now the prize coveted by all. The mighty Spanish Empire with its silver, its armaments, ships, cargoes and political conceptions, now turned towards that immense battlefield. At the same moment in time, the Ottomans turned their backs firmly on the Mediterranean to plunge into conflict on the Asian border. This should remind us . . . that the two great Mediterranean Empires beat with the same rhythm and that at least during the last twenty years of the century, the Mediterranean itself was no longer the focus of their ambitions and desires.

Fernand Braudel, *The Mediterranean and the Mediterranean World in the Age of Philip II*, trans. S. Reynolds, vol II, 1972, pp 676–8

Questions

a   What reasons does the author give for Philip II's 'withdrawal to Spain' (line 16)? What were the consequences of this 'withdrawal'?

b   What was the chief practical disadvantage of the 'growth of a sedentary administration' (lines 27–8)?

c   What was 'the financial disaster of 1557' (line 38)? What were its chief results?

d   Who was Granvelle (line 46)? What does the author imply was the result of his return?

* e   Who, in the long run, did win 'control of the Atlantic Ocean' (line 50)?

* f   Can you suggest any reasons why the Spanish and Ottomans both 'turned their backs firmly on the Mediterranean' (line 56) at this time?

IX The Revolt of the Netherlands

Introduction

The revolt of the Netherlands was one of the few rebellions in the sixteenth century which was not quickly suppressed. It had a number of causes, not only the political and religious ones mentioned by King Philip II of Spain (extract 1), but also economic causes, which no contemporary really appreciated. These included Philip's first bankruptcy in 1557, which ruined many Antwerp merchants, and the unemployment and bad harvests of the 1560s, which caused distress, particularly to urban workers, who were a more important part of the population in Flanders and Brabant than in other parts of Europe.

The character and temperament of Philip himself, too, influenced events because he was so unsympathetic to the traditions and aspirations of the Netherlanders, especially in the matter of religion. The spread of Protestantism, and in particular of militant Calvinism, was of great importance; without it there might have been no revolt, and it was religion which linked the revolt with events in France and other parts of Europe.

What actually happened was a complex series of military and political moves, with the provinces united in opposition to Spain, but generally in nothing else. This was one reason for the signing of the Pacification of Ghent, a temporary measure, whose failure was underlined by the formation of the Unions of Utrecht and Arras in 1579.

The division of the Netherlands into the independent United Provinces and the Southern Spanish Netherlands was not foreseen by anyone in the sixteenth century. Since the 1930s the customary explanation for this division has been the one provided by Pieter Geyl (extract 6), but there are a number of other reasons for it, as the last extracts in this section illustrate.

Further Reading

Pieter Geyl, *The Revolt of the Netherlands 1555 – 1609* (Ernest Benn, 1966)
Edward Grierson, *The Fatal Inheritance* (Gollancz, 1969)
Geoffrey Parker, *The Dutch Revolt* (Allen Lane, 1977)
C. V. Wedgwood, *William the Silent* (Cape, 1944)
Charles Wilson, *Queen Elizabeth and the Revolt of the Netherlands* (University of California Press, 1970)

1 Philip II to the Duchess of Parma

Since my last letters of 6 May I have received several letters. . . . All of them tell me of the great troubles and disturbances stirred up in the Netherlands to my regret, on the pretext of religion, after some confederates presented to you a petition in which they called the
5 inquisition in question and asked to abolish the religious edicts and to draft others in collaboration with the States General, and to suspend the execution of both inquisition and edicts until I shall have made my decision. . . .

To remedy this you told me earlier that your advisers saw only two
10 possibilities, namely to take up arms (which would be very difficult) or to give in on some points, to abolish the inquisition and to moderate the rigour of the edicts little by little. . . .

What is at stake is on the one hand the respect for our holy Catholic faith which I have always had at heart and furthered with due zeal and in
15 accordance with the obligation I have to maintain it; on the other hand I fear that great difficulties and trouble might come to so many of the honest vassals and subjects whom I have in the Low Countries.

The inquisition was originally introduced into my territories . . . because there were not enough bishops then and because the persons in
20 charge were negligent, I feel that the situation is now different. . . . As the episcopal jurisdiction is now fully and firmly established I am content for the inquisition to cease. . . .

But I have always been inclined to treat my vassals and subjects with the utmost clemency, abhorring nothing so much as the use of severity
25 when things may be remedied in another way. If therefore you see that the difficulties are being overcome by means of the above-mentioned measures and that a general pardon would be the final measure to pacify the country, I grant you permission to give it in the form and way you think best.

> Philip II, from Segovia, 31 July 1566, in E. H. Kossman and A. F. Mellink, *Texts Concerning the Revolt of the Netherlands*, 1974, pp 69–74

Questions

a   What were the subject of (i) the 'petition' (line 4) and (ii) 'the religious edicts' (line 5)? Who were the 'confederates' (line 4)?

b   Explain the reference to 'not enough bishops' and 'the episcopal jurisdiction . . . now fully and firmly established' (lines 19–21).

* c   Why was the inquisition so much disliked in the Netherlands?

* d   Why did Philip decide to change from a policy of 'clemency' to one of 'severity' (line 24)? What actions were taken as a result of this change of policy?

* e   What factors, not referred to in this letter, also contributed to the outbreak of the revolt of the Netherlands?

f How had Philip tried to 'further' the 'holy Catholic faith' (lines 13–14) in the Netherlands?

2 The Pacification of Ghent

In order that total ruin may be staved off, that the inhabitants of all these Netherlands united in a lasting peace and agreement may jointly force the Spaniards and their adherents, who are a public plague, to depart and that they may be given back their old privileges, customs and freedoms, by
5 which trade and prosperity could return there, now, with the consent of the councillors entrusted with the government of the countries . . . this present treaty has been drafted between . . . Brabant, Flanders, Hainault [etc.] . . . representing the States of those countries, and the prince of Orange, the States of Holland, Zeeland and their associates. . . .
10 II In consequence the said states of Brabant, Flanders, Hainault, etc., as well as the Prince, the States of Holland and Zeeland with their associates promise sincerely and honestly to keep, and oblige all inhabitants of the provinces to maintain, from now on a lasting and unbreakable friendship and peace and to assist each other at all times and in all events by words
15 and deeds, with their lives and property, and to drive and keep out of the provinces the Spanish soldiers.
III . . . Immediately after the departure of the Spaniards and their adherents and after law and order has been restored, the two parties will be bound to do their utmost to convoke an assembly of the States
20 General. . . . The assembly must settle the affairs of the provinces in general and in detail, not only the matter and exercise of religion in Holland, Zeeland, Bommel and associated places. . . .
v In the meantime no one may be lightly accused, arrested or endangered; all edicts about heresy formerly made and promulgated, as well as the
25 criminal ordinance made by the duke of Alva, shall be suspended.

The Pacification of Ghent, 8 November 1576, in E. H. Kossman and A. F. Mellink, *Texts Concerning the Revolt of the Netherlands*, 1974, pp 126–8

Questions

a Why were 'councillors entrusted with the government' (line 6)?
b Why was a treaty necessary between Brabant, etc., and the prince of Orange, Holland and Zeeland?
c What was the States General? Why was it necessary for it to settle 'the matter and exercise of religion' (line 21)?
d What was the purpose of Alva's 'criminal ordinance' (line 25)?
* *e* What prompted the representatives of the provinces to agree to this document?
* *f* Why did the Pacification fail to achieve its purpose of uniting all the Netherlanders against Spain?

3   The Union of Utrecht

It is clear that since the conclusion of the Pacification of Ghent, according
to which nearly all the provinces of these Low Countries undertook to
assist each other with their life and property in driving the
Spaniards . . . from this country, the Spaniards as well as Don John of
5 Austria . . . have sought and are still seeking by all means in their power
to bring these provinces wholly or partly into subjection under their
tyrannical government and into slavery. . . . So those from the duchy of
Gelderland and the county of Zutphen, and those from . . . Holland,
Zeeland, Utrecht and the Ommelanden . . . have thought it advisable to
10 ally and to unite more closely and particularly, not with the intention of
withdrawing from . . . the Pacification of Ghent but rather to strengthen
it and to protect themselves against all the difficulties that their enemy's
practices, attacks or outrages might bring upon them. . . .
i   The afore-said provinces shall ally, confederate and unite . . . to hold
15 together eternally in all ways and forms as if they were one province. . . . However, this is agreed without prejudice to the special and
particular privileges, freedoms, exemptions, laws, statutes, laudable and
traditional customs, usages and all other rights of each province and of
each town, member and inhabitant of those provinces. Not only shall the
20 provinces not hinder each other from exercising those rights . . . but
they shall help each other by all proper and possible means to maintain
and strengthen them. . . .
XIII   Concerning the matter of religion: Holland and Zeeland shall act at
their own discretion whereas the other provinces of this Union . . . may
25 introduce . . . such regulations as they consider proper for the peace and
welfare of the provinces . . . and for the preservation of all
people . . . provided that in accordance with the Pacification of Ghent
each individual enjoys freedom of religion and no one is persecuted or
questioned about his religion.

> Treaty of the Union, eternal alliance and confederation made in
> the town of Utrecht by the countries and their towns and
> members, 29 January 1579, in E. H. Kossman and A. F. Mellink,
> *Texts Concerning the Revolt of the Netherlands*, 1974, pp 165-70

Questions

a How was Don John trying 'to bring these provinces . . . into
subjection' (line 6), thus making the formation of this Union
necessary?

b How did the position of Holland and Zeeland differ from that of the
other signatory provinces 'concerning the matter of religion' (line
23)?

* c Do you think it would ever have been possible to reconcile fully the
first sentence of clause I with the rest of the clause? How did this later
cause problems for the United Provinces?

* *d* Why did the Union of Utrecht *not* 'strengthen' the Pacification of Ghent (lines 11–12)?

4 The Outlawing of William of Orange

It is well known to all how favourably the late emperor, Charles the Fifth, . . . treated William of Nassau, . . . and how, from William's earliest youth, he promoted his advancement, as we . . . have continued to do. By reason of this and the oaths of fidelity and homage taken to us,

5 he was specially bound to us, and under obligation to obey and keep faith with us and safeguard our interests and to do all in his power to secure peace and tranquillity in our several dominions and provinces. He was the instigator and chief author of the first protest which was presented by certain young gentlemen who daily frequented his house and table.

10 Moreover, with the knowledge, advice and encouragement of the said Orange, the heretics commenced to destroy the images, altars and churches in a disorderly manner, and to desecrate all holy and sacred objects, especially the sacraments ordained of God. . . .

Then he introduced liberty of conscience, or to speak more correctly,

15 confusion of all religion, which soon brought it about that the Catholics were openly persecuted and driven out. . . . Moreover he obtained such a hold upon our poor subjects of Holland and Zeeland and brought affairs to such a pass that nearly all the towns, one after the other, have been besieged and taken. . . .

20 Therefore, for all these just reasons, for his evil doings as chief disturber of the public peace and as a public pest, we outlaw him forever and forbid all our subjects to associate with him or communicate with him. . . . We promise, on the word of a king and as God's servant, that if one of our subjects be found so generous of heart and so desirous of doing us a

25 service . . . that he shall find means of ridding us of the said pest, either by delivering him to us dead or alive, or by depriving him at once of life, we will give him . . . the amount of twenty-five thousand gold crowns.

Proclamation of Philip II, 1580, in J. H. Robinson, *Readings in European History*, vol II, pp 174–7

Questions

a Why is the prince of Orange described as 'William of Nassau' (line 2)?

b Who was really to blame for (i) 'the first protest' (line 8), (ii) the destruction of 'images, altars and churches' (lines 11–12) and (iii) the siege and capture of towns?

* *c* In what sense was it accurate to describe William as 'chief disturber of the public peace' (lines 20–21)?

d How had William 'obtained such a hold upon our poor subjects of Holland and Zeeland' (lines 16–17)?

* *e* What evidence is there that most Netherlanders, in the northern

provinces at least, preferred to be ruled by William rather than by Spain?

5 Iconoclasm

The Netherlands possessed an extraordinary number of churches and monasteries. . . . All were peopled with statues. All were filled with profusely-adorned chapels. . . .

5   And now [1566], for the space of only six or seven summer days and nights, there raged a storm by which all those treasures were destroyed. Nearly every one of these temples was entirely rifled of its contents; not for the purpose of plunder, but of destruction. Hardly a province or a town escaped. . . .

The movement was a sudden explosion of popular revenge against the
10   symbols of that Church by which the Reformers had been enduring such terrible persecution. It was also an expression of the general sympathy for the doctrines which had taken possession of the national heart. . . .

The effect of the riots was destined to be most disastrous for a time to the reforming party. It furnished plausible excuses for many lukewarm
15   friends of their cause to withdraw from all connection with it. . . . The sublime spectacle of the multitudinous field-preaching was sullied by the excesses of the image-breaking. The religious war, before imminent, became inevitable.

Nevertheless, the first effect of the tumults was a temporary advantage
20   to the Reformers. A great concession was extorted from the fears of the Duchess Regent, who was certainly placed in a terrible position. . . .

The important Accord was then duly signed by the Duchess. It declared that the inquisition was abolished, that his Majesty would soon issue a new general edict, expressly and unequivocally protecting the
25   nobles against all evil consequences from past transactions, that they were to be employed in the royal service, and that public preaching according to the forms of the new religion was to be practised in places where it had already taken place.

J. L. Motley, *The Rise of the Dutch Republic*, vol I, 1862, pp 464–5, 479–82, 485

Questions

a   Who were 'the Duchess Regent' (line 21) and 'his Majesty' (line 23)? What is meant by 'the Reformers' (line 10)?
b   Why did the iconoclasts take the action described in the second and third paragraphs?
c   What was the 'disastrous' result (line 13) of this action?
d   Why was 'field-preaching' (line 16) necessary and why was it so effective?
*   e   How significant was the Duchess' 'great concession' (line 20)? What

influence did it have on subsequent Spanish policy towards the Netherlands?

f Why were special arrangements made for the nobles in 'the important Accord' (line 22)?

6 The Importance of the Rivers

It is unnecessary to subject to a set criticism the view, which has long been current, and according to which the split was determined by some inherent divergence between the Netherlands people. A Protestant North (not without numerous Catholics however) and a Catholic South
5   were not predetermined by the natures of the populations. Those two great cultural currents of Catholicism and Protestantism originally mingled their courses in both North and South. It was only the outcome of strife, of war with the foreign ruler, which brought about that fatal redistribution of forces which was to estrange the two regions for so long.
10 That outcome was not determined by any greater courage possessed by the North, or even by Holland and Zeeland alone (for the conventional view conveniently overlooks the fact that the eastern provinces had to be reconquered for the Republic by force). That outcome was determined by the great rivers. Brabant and Flanders lay open for the enemy, and
15 soon therefore their Protestants went to strengthen those in the impregnable river area. Gelderland, Overysel and Groningen, much less affected by Protestantism than Flanders and Brabant, could not be held for the Catholic Church because the swords of Parma and of Spinola lost their striking-force when stretched precariously beyond the rivers.

Pieter Geyl, *The Revolt of the Netherlands*, 1958, p 256

Questions

a Name 'the great rivers' (line 14). What was the countryside like beside and between them?
b If the division of the Netherlands had been decided solely on the basis of religion, approximately where would the boundary have been drawn?
*   *c* What evidence is there, in this passage or elsewhere, to support Geyl's theory about the division of the Netherlands?
*   *d* What other factors contributed to the outcome of the Revolt?

7 Queen Elizabeth and the Revolt of the Netherlands

The Treaty of Nonsuch of 1585 committed Elizabeth to maintain a sizeable English Army in the Netherlands. Five thousand foot and a thousand horse were to serve at the Queen's expense – temporarily. . . . By way of security for the costs incurred, the strategically vital ports of

5   Flushing and The Brill were to remain in English hands and be garrisoned at the Queen's expense. What the Queen would not do was to accept the sovereignty of the rebel provinces.

Three months later, in November, she felt moved to issue a declaration to the world justifying her final departure from ten years of attempted benevolent neutrality. In versions published simultaneously in English, Dutch, French and Italian, she declared her unshakeable devotion to the ancient Burgundian alliance, while denouncing Spanish atrocities committed not·only against Protestant subjects but against Catholics too. Conveniently oblivious of her earlier refusal to lift a finger to help Egmont, she referred particularly to him who, of all the nobility maltreated by the King, had deserved best of Spain and been most cruelly victimised as a loyal subject and a Catholic. The Netherlands themselves had been laid waste, but it was not only the Netherlands against which Philip had offended. She herself and her realm had been the target for conspiracies in England, Ireland and Scotland. Her aims were threefold: a general peace; the recognition of religious freedom and the restoration of the ancient liberties of the Netherlands; and security for England, which could only enjoy tranquillity when the Low Countries were tranquil. It might have been a declaration by Orange himself. . . .

Inadvertently, but only so, the future constitution of the Dutch republic emerged from the follies and failures of English policy in the seventies and eighties. The lingering obsession for a foreign sovereign which had characterised Netherlands policies and diplomacy for twenty years was at last dispelled. Under Oldenbarneveldt and Maurice of Nassau the States could set their feet on a path towards genuine independence. The most that could be said for the English intervention before the Armada was that, in spite of the betrayals and failures, it had probably helped to slow down Farnese's advance northwards. More important, the lessons learnt at terrible cost by the English commanders were to be increasingly valuable during the next twenty years. . . .

Conservatism, parsimony, snobbery, distrust: these explain [Elizabeth's] refusal to commit herself down to 1585. By then it was too late to save the unity of the Netherlands. Her attitude to the Dutch changed only as their successes in the nineties proved even to the Queen that she had miscalculated their capacity not only to survive but to prosper. The Treaty of Nonsuch had pitched her into heavy expenses which (as Philip Sidney observed) might have been avoided if she had listened to her advisers earlier; and this at a time when the national finances were less able to bear them. . . . Yet the real gravamen of the charge against the Queen does not relate to the Leicester period, gross though the mismanagement of it was. The worst damage was inflicted between 1575 and 1579 (and perhaps 1585), when the prospect of a united Netherlands beckoned. It was the view of a majority of her ministers throughout these years, and during at least three crises the unanimous view of all the ministers concerned (including even Burghley) that it was urgently necessary to send immediate and effective aid to the Netherlands. The Queen herself

accepted this policy. She professed to regard William as the only salvation of the Netherlands and implicitly accepted his argument (always shared by many of her advisers and more than once by all) that the security and
55　prosperity of England was indissolubly bound up with that of a united Netherlands. Yet on each occasion when the moment of decision arrived, she suffered one of her characteristic last-minute ·blackouts. . . .

Her policy, or lack of it, contributed to the disintegration of that [Netherlands] society, to the drift first of both North and South towards
60　France, then of the South back to Spain. Without the seduction of the Walloon nobility by Parma, the great Spanish enterprise against England would have been impossible. Assured of their support and deploying the newly recalled Spanish army, Parma was far stronger than any of his predecessors had been. The truth of William's reiterated conviction was
65　now inescapable. The threat to the Netherlands and the threat to England were inseparably connected, two halves of a single strategy.

Charles Wilson, *Queen Elizabeth and the Revolt of the Netherlands*, 1970, pp 86–7, 103, 128–9, 134

Questions

a　Explain the reference to the 'Burgundian alliance' (line 12).
b　Why had Egmont been 'victimised' and why had he 'deserved best of Spain' (lines 16–17)?
*　*c*　Explain the parts in the government of the Northern provinces taken by Oldenbarneveldt and Maurice of Nassau after 1585.
d　How, according to the author, did Elizabeth's policies help to make the Armada possible?
*　*e*　What is the charge which the author is making against Queen Elizabeth? What evidence is there to support it?

8　The Importance of Finance

Hapsburg Spain was, in the sixteenth century, unquestionably the most powerful state in Western Europe. The revenues, dominions and armies of the King of Spain were by far the largest of any European potentate. Yet the very dimensions and daunting resources of the empire excited
5　enmity. Spain's three imperial holdings in Europe – the Low Countries, much of Italy and finally Portugal – brought her sooner or later into open conflict with three other powers: England, France and the Ottoman Sultan. The Spanish kings were rich, but they did not control anything approaching the resources required to fight all three enemies at once, let
10　alone to suppress simultaneously any domestic unrest, and therefore Spain was for ever balancing the needs of defence or action in one area against the needs of the others. There had to be a table of imperial priorities, a set of criteria which enabled the central government to decide how best to allocate its inadequate resources. . . .

15   It would not seem that the level of expenditure was in any way
     determined . . . by the available revenues or the state of the
     economy. . . . This is not to say, however, that governments spent their
     money without *any* preconceived plan. . . . It emerges, moreover, that
     the priorities which affected the Netherlands were fairly simple, and
20   changed little in the course of the Eighty Years War.

     It is clear that at the top of Spain's priorities came her fear of France.
     Any war which involved France, even covertly, became of paramount
     importance. . . . It was therefore inevitable that the Netherlands would
     suffer if Spain became involved in any war which also concerned France.

25   The other major question of imperial policy which clearly involved
     the Netherlands was the defence of Italy. There were always some
     councillors at the court of Spain who believed that the security of Italy
     and the war against the Turks at sea should be subordinated to the defence
     of the Netherlands and the war against the heretics; there were always
30   some councillors of the opposite persuasion. . . .

     It was simple political choices such as these which, more than anything
     else, determined the course of the war in the Netherlands because, far
     more than tax-yields, they governed the immediate level of Spanish
     expenditure there and elsewhere.

> Geoffrey Parker, *Spain, Her Enemies and the Revolt of the
> Netherlands 1559–1648*, Past and Present, no. 49, 1970, pp 73,
> 93–5

Questions

a What is the author arguing here about the reasons for Spain's loss of
     the Netherlands?

b What evidence is there that 'the defence of the Netherlands' was
     affected by 'the war against the Turks' (lines 28–9)?

* *c* How did the duke of Alva endeavour to overcome this financial
     problem and why did he fail?

* *d* Why and how did (i) 'fear of France' (line 21) and (ii) conflict with
     England affect developments in the Netherlands?

9   Mutiny in the Spanish Armies

Like most civilian revolts of the early modern period, the military
mutinies of the Spanish army reveal no evidence of any revolutionary
purpose or politically conscious agitators. There is not a hint that any
mutineers dreamed of overturning the established order, none that they
5   even wished to influence the government towards making peace. . . .
The mutineers were indeed more like strikers: they wanted to receive the
wages they had already earned and a formal promise of better conditions
of service in the future.

Nevertheless, the mutinies of the Spanish army in the Netherlands

10   certainly did not lack political significance. Because they tied down the
government's élite troops and involved such vast amounts of money, the
outbreak of a major military revolt usually paralysed the army for a
whole campaign, sabotaging any offensive and jeopardising the security
of loyal but isolated towns. In certain circumstances a mutiny could
15   undermine the very foundations of the government's authority. In 1574
the Spanish Governor-General of the Netherlands, Don Luis de
Requesens, lamented that the mutiny of his most seasoned troops at
Antwerp called into question the whole basis of Spanish power. . . .
        On Sunday 4 November [1576] the Spaniards carried out a surprise
20   attack on the city [Antwerp]. Beneath their banner, which displayed
Christ on the Cross on one side and the Madonna on the other, the
mutineers stormed the city and sacked it. Eight thousand civilians were
killed, often in the most barbarous manner, and perhaps one thousand
houses were destroyed in this desperate action, known to posterity as the
25   'Spanish Fury'.
        The terrible holocaust . . . destroyed the last vestiges of the king's
authority in the Netherlands. On 8 November the 'Pacification of Ghent'
was ratified by representatives of almost all the provinces of the Low
Countries, again without reference to the king, bringing the war to an
30   end. The sack of the richest city in Northern Europe convinced every
Netherlander that peace had to be secured immediately and at all costs.
Philip II's mutinous troops might have taken Antwerp, but they had lost
the Netherlands in doing so.

> Geoffrey Parker, *Mutiny and Discontent in the Spanish Army of*
> *Flanders 1572–1607*, Past and Present, no. 58, 1973, pp 47–9

Questions

a   What argument is the author putting forward here to explain Spain's
      loss of the Netherlands?
*
b   What made the sack of Antwerp more important than other mutinies
      by the Spanish army?
*
c   Why did Spanish troops need to mutiny so often to force the payment
      of their wages?

d   Why did Requesens believe that mutiny 'called into question the
      whole basis of Spanish power' (lines 17–18)?

X   The French Wars of Religion

Introduction

The French wars of religion are one of the most confused and confusing episodes in sixteenth-century history. Beginning with the massacre at Vassy, they were marked throughout by unnecessary violence and atrocities and ended with an exhausted and partly devastated country.

One important cause of war was religion – the extent to which protestants could be allowed freedom of worship, if at all, was a constant theme and one which could never be settled to the satisfaction of both sides. Other issues became associated with it, in particular the question of who should control the king, especially during Charles IX's minority, and thus whether the Roman Catholics or the Huguenots should be in command of the country. As an expression of this, some of the nobles, such as the prince de Condé, who were strongly opposed to the leading catholic family, the Guises, used their protestantism to indicate their political position.

The most controversial character in the wars was undoubtedly Catherine de Medici (extract 3). Her religious position was never made absolutely clear, and her attempts to rule the country effectively were resented by both sides. When her son Charles, under the influence of Coligny, Louis of Nassau and others, agreed to help the Dutch rebels in 1572 she decided the moment for decisive action had come and arranged for Coligny's murder. The failure of the first attempt led to the massacre of St Bartholomew (extract 4), but this in fact settled nothing – except that the French were then unable to help the Dutch.

Indeed, the final outcome of the wars, as expressed in the Edict of Nantes (extract 7), might have been reached in the early stages, if all sides had been prepared to compromise.

Further Reading

Robin Briggs, *Early Modern France 1560–1715* (Oxford University Press, 1977)

D. Buisseret, *Huguenots and Papists* (Ginn, 1972)

Desmond Seward, *The First Bourbon* (Constable, 1971)

N. M. Sutherland, *The Massacre of St Bartholomew and the European Conflict, 1559–1572* (Macmillan, 1973)

1 The Causes of the Wars of Religion

The unexpected death of Henry II in 1559 provided the opportunity for
simmering discontent to break out into the open. His successor, Francis II,
was only fifteen years old and incapable of exerting the personal authority
necessary to deflect the opposition. It was something of a paradox in fact
5   that the antagonism inspired by the Crown's more public, less personal
image could only be expressed openly when the ruler himself lacked the
strength of personality to enforce his authority. That was because the
French monarch . . . traditionally maintained a formidable hold over his
subjects' minds so that when the crisis came, and one youthful and
10   inadequate ruler succeeded another, the issue long remained in
doubt. . . .

The three inter-related elements which provoked that struggle all
stemmed, directly or indirectly, from the same root cause: the changing
nature of government which no longer seemed willing either to
15   guarantee the *status quo* or to delimit the area of its intervention. First,
there was the loss of status affecting powerful, princely and aristocratic
families whose former relationship had allowed them direct access to the
monarch, but who now found themselves removed, at one step, as legal,
financial and administrative experts were summoned increasingly to cope
20   with expanding government business. . . .

The Italian wars of Francis I and Henry II had been expensive and the
burden of the *taille*, a direct tax on persons, and, in some cases, on land,
crippling on many of the unprivileged class who had to pay it. The
ramifications of this fact were felt higher up the social scale, for the
25   impoverished tenants could not pay their feudal dues. . . . Additionally,
the noble class had made unprecedented financial contributions to the war
effort. . . .

Such discontent in so many quarters presented a serious enough
problem for the youthful Francis II and his mother, Catherine de Medici,
30   but when the third, and much the most significant element, that of
religious dissent, was joined to the other two, the French crown was
confronted with a veritable crisis of confidence.

J. H. Shennan, *The Origins of the Modern European State 1450–
1725*, 1974, pp 69–71

Questions

a   Explain the reference to 'the Crown's more public, less personal
*   image' (lines 5–6).

b   Which of the great families of France were still trying to maintain
their powerful position in the government at this time? Why did this
matter?

*

c   What was the nature of 'religious dissent' (line 31) in France? Why
*   was it such a problem for the government?

d   What were the other causes of the wars of religion? What actually led
to the outbreak of war in 1562?

2   The Outbreak of the Wars of Religion

A single event set fire to the powder train. On 1st March 1562 the duc de
Guise was passing through Vassy when he heard that some Protestants
were conducting a service in a barn. If the barn in question was, as seems
likely, actually situated in the town, this was an act of imprudence, for the
5   Edict of January gave the Protestants the right to celebrate their cult
outside towns only. Whatever the rights of the matter, the Duke's
soldiers fell upon the congregation and massacred the participants. . . .

    The news of the massacre caused a great stir within Protestant circles in
the capital. Beza went at once to the Queen to demand that justice be
10 done. The King of Navarre, who was present at the interview, defended
the duc de Guise. . . .

    Despite the Queen's orders, Guise made a triumphal entry to Paris and
was immediately joined by the King of Navarre. The Queen appealed to
Condé and asked him to take the young King and herself under his
15 protection. Condé acted evasively and made no effort to prevent the duc
de Guise reaching Fontainebleau, where the court was located. Relying
on the repeated demands of Catherine de Medici Condé then declared the
young king to be the prisoner of the Guises. On 12th April he issued a call
to arms to the Protestant churches.

20 Many towns joined the reformed party in answer to Condé's
appeal. . . . But few of them sent troops to reinforce the army that
Condé had concentrated at Orleans. Catherine de Medici attempted
conciliation, but the Triumvirs insisted that the King 'should neither
approve nor suffer any diversity of religion in his kingdom'. . . . By July
25 it was clear that there could be no other outcome but war.

      Samuel Mours, *Le Protestantisme en France au seizième siecle*, 1959,
      in J. H. M. Salmon, *The French Wars of Religion*, 1967, pp 11 – 13

Questions

a What was the legal position of Protestant worship after 'the Edict of
    January' (line 5)? In what way may the Protestants at Vassy have been
    violating it?

b Who was Beza (line 9)? What was the significance of his presence at
    the French court?

c Who was 'the King of Navarre' (line 10)? Why was he one of the
    leading figures at the French court and why was his association with
    Guise unexpected?

d Is it possible to explain Condé's actions at this time?

e Was there any way in which war could have been avoided once the
    massacre at Vassy had occurred?

3   Catherine de Medici

As to the queen, it is enough to say that she is a woman, but, I should add, a foreigner as well, and even more, a Florentine, born in a private family, very unequal to the grandeur of the kingdom of France. On this account she does not have the reputation or authority which she would have, perhaps, if she had been born in the kingdom or of more illustrious blood. It cannot be denied that she is a woman of great worth and intelligence; and if she had greater experience in matters of state, and were a bit more firm, she might well achieve great things. But in the time of King Henry, her husband, she was held down; and although after the succession of King Francis she seemed to have supreme authority, it was only apparently so because the Cardinal of Lorraine did everything by himself. For this reason her Majesty has need of good advisers, but she has no one in whom she can trust; dissension in religion and discord among the great have made everyone suspect to her. . . .

As for the intentions of her Majesty in matters of religion, opinions differ. . . . I can affirm, however, from what I have seen, although I do not know what her Majesty's true sentiments are, that she does not suffer willingly these tumults in the kingdom. If she has not shown herself as zealous in repressing them as one could desire, she has been restrained by fear that the necessity of using force would tear France to pieces. . . . I know that she is trying to hold all her sons safely in the Catholic faith and in Christian ways of life; she speaks earnestly to this effect with many persons. And therefore I believe that one should think well of her Majesty rather than otherwise. If her actions do not bear out her desires, the reason is perhaps that she does not have all the authority or experience that are needed.

> Report of Michele Suriano, Venetian ambassador, 1561, in J. B. Ross and M. M. McLaughlin, *The Portable Renaissance Reader*, 1977, pp 324–5

Questions

a   Why was the queen in such a powerful position in 1561?

b   Who was 'the Cardinal of Lorraine' (line 11)? Why had he been so important during the previous reign?

*   c   What were the causes of the 'dissension in religion and discord among the great' (line 13)? What effect did these have on the government of France?

*   d   Why should there be doubt about the queen's intentions with regard to her sons' religion?

*   e   What can be regarded as Catherine de Medici's greatest achievements? What was her greatest failure?

4   The Massacre of St Bartholomew

On Thursday, 27th [*sic*] August, at eleven in the morning, the Admiral, having left the palace, stopped to read a letter that a Huguenot gentleman had just given him, at some fifty or sixty paces from the palace. From a neighbouring house he was hit by an arquebus shot, which carried away one finger of his right hand and went through his arm and left hand. . . .

That day and the next, it was widely said among the Huguenots that the Most Christian King or the Duke of Anjou were not strangers to this attempt; they further said that it had been committed by order of the dukes of Guise and Aumale, or of the Duke of Alba. . . .

On Sunday, Saint Bartholomew's day, at three o'clock in the morning, the alarm was rung; all the Parisians began killing the Huguenots of the town, breaking down the doors of the houses in which they lived and pillaging what they found within.

The said Guise, Aumale and Angoulême went to the Admiral's house, which they entered. . . . They went up to his room, and in the bed in which he was lying, the Duke of Guise shot him in the head with a pistol; then they took him and threw him naked out of the window into the courtyard of his house. . . .

The massacre lasted until the morning of Tuesday, 25th August.

On this day, the Most Christian King, dressed in his royal robes, went to the palace and declared to the parliament that he had been obliged to make the peace that he had made with the Huguenots because his people were exhausted and ruined, but that now that God had given him victory over his enemies . . . he desired that the edict that he had formerly published should be observed, according to which no other religion than the Catholic, Apostolic and Roman might be practised in the kingdom. . . .

The princes of Béarn [Navarre] and Condé are utterly downcast: they dare not say a word, and an official . . . [said] that on the 27th they went to mass with the king.

> From the report of Juan de Olaegui, the Spanish ambassador's secretary, 1572, in P. Erlanger, *St Bartholomew's Night*, 1962, pp 240–4

Questions

a   Who were (i) 'the Admiral' (line 1) and (ii) the 'most Christian king' (line 7)?

*   b   Why might (i) the Duke of Guise and (ii) the Duke of Alba be suspected of involvement in the attempted murder?

*   c   Which leading figure at the French court is rather surprisingly not mentioned in this account? What part had this person played?

d   Why could it be said that 'all the Parisians' (line 11) were involved in the massacre and why were so many Huguenots in Paris at this time?

*   e   What were the details of the peace which the king had 'been obliged to make' (lines 21–2)?

f   Explain the reference to Navarre and Condé in the last paragraph.

5 An Attempt to Restore Order

Monsieur de Rambouillet. Upon my arrival in this kingdom I declared and made known . . . my singular desire and intention to look to the tranquillity of my kingdom and the security and preservation of all my subjects who have been or still may be of the new party [Huguenots]
5 when they behave as they should; in so doing, I would have thought that I had thereby provided at least the chief and principal remedies for bringing about a settlement of the war and divisions which currently disunite my subjects. Nevertheless, although those who have revolted ought to renounce their evil undertaking and give me the obedience they
10 owe, on the contrary they have urged others who are peacefully residing in their houses, and are still urging them, to act like them and thus strengthen their party, and to this end they have circulated a number of false rumours, succeeding thereby − so I have heard − in stirring some of the most docile into revolt and the taking up of arms, as the continual
15 meetings, comings and goings between each other's houses, the marches of armed bands by night and the sale of their produce and personal property, demonstrate well enough. To deal with this situation, I have decided to write this letter to tell you that in accordance with my honest and sincere intention . . . I wish you to continue to assure all those who
20 have been or may still be of the new party and who remain in their homes, and others who may be in a state of fear and distrust, that I have no other wish than to maintain and preserve the security of their lives and possessions so long as they remain quietly in their houses without undertaking anything contrary to the good of my service. But if you
25 discover . . . anybody seeking to act in a manner prejudicial to my service, it is my wish that before they have time to do so, especially those who move by night and with arms, whose intentions may be mischievous, you should fall upon them as rebels.

Henry III to the Seigneur de Rambouillet, from Avignon, 29 November 1574, in J. H. Shennan, *Government and Society in France 1461−1661*, 1969, pp 130−1

Questions

a Why does Henry begin 'upon my arrival in this kingdom' (line 1)?

b As Monsieur de Rambouillet was lieutenant-general of Maine, what responsibilities did he have which explain why the king wrote to him in this way?

* c Why was it unlikely that M. de Rambouillet would be able to carry out the king's orders effectively?

* d Why was the action proposed in this letter unlikely to satisfy the Huguenots?

* e Why had the Huguenots been acting in the way described and what did they really want?

6 A Huguenot Encourages Rebellion

It is, then, not only lawful for Israel to resist a king who overturns the Law and the Church of God, but if they do not do so, they are guilty of the same crime and are subject to the same penalty. . . . When we speak of the people collectively, we mean those who receive authority from the
5 people. . . .

In every properly constituted kingdom, this is the character of the officers of the crown, the peers, the lords, the patricians, the notables and others chosen by the several estates who, in various combinations, make up the membership of the . . . council. . . . The office of all these is to see
10 that no harm is suffered either by the commonwealth or by the Church. For although these officers are severally below the king, they are collectively above him. . . . Since, therefore, good government depends on a degree of order that cannot be maintained in a large multitude, and since affairs of state often cannot be communicated publicly without
15 danger to the common interest, everything that we have maintained was granted and entrusted to the people as a whole applies rather to the officers of the kingdom. . . .

We have shown that the people as a whole, or the officers of the kingdom whom the people have established, or the majority of these, or
20 any one of them, very gravely sin against the covenant with God if they do not use force against a king who corrupts God's law or prevents its restoration, in order to confine him to his proper bounds. Residents of towns and provinces, which are the individual parts of a kingdom, are subject to the same penalty if they do not at least drive idolatry beyond
25 their borders, when the ruler seeks to introduce it, and maintain true doctrine by whatever means they can, even if it means seceding temporarily at some point.

> Philippe du Plessis-Mornay, *Vindiciae contra Tyrannos*, 1579, in J. H. Franklin, *Constitutionalism and Resistance in the Sixteenth Century*, 1969, pp 149– 50, 157– 8

Questions

a To whom does the author apply the name 'Israel' (line 1)? What does he mean by 'idolatry' (line 24)?

b What does he believe justifies rebellion against a king and of which section of society is this the special responsibility?

c Why cannot the decision to resist the king be taken by the people as a whole?

* d Which 'towns and provinces' of France in the 1570s and 1580s tried to 'drive idolatry beyond their borders' (lines 23– 5)? Could this be described as 'seceding temporarily' (lines 26– 7)?

* e How does the author's attitude to 'a king who corrupts God's law' (line 21) compare with that of Calvin, of whom he was a follower (extract 4 in section VI)?

7 The Edict of Nantes, 1598

Among the infinite benefits which it has pleased God to heap upon us, the most signal and precious is his granting us the strength and ability to withstand the fearful disorders and troubles which prevailed on our advent in this kingdom. The realm was so torn by innumerable factions
5 and sects that the most legitimate of all the parties was fewest in numbers. God has given us strength to stand out against this storm; we have finally surmounted the waves and made our port of safety – peace for our state. . . .

We have, by this perpetual and irrevocable edict, established and
10 proclaimed and do establish and proclaim. . . .

III We ordain that the Catholic Apostolic and Roman religion shall be restored and re-established in all places and localities of this our kingdom and countries subject to our sway, where the exercise of the same has been interrupted, in order that it may be peaceably and freely exercised,
15 without any trouble and hindrance. . . .

VI And in order to leave no occasion for troubles or differences between our subjects, we have permitted, and herewith permit, those of the said religion called Reformed to live and abide in all the cities and places of this our kingdom and countries of our sway, without being annoyed,
20 molested, or compelled to do anything in the matter of religion contrary to their consciences. . . .

IX We also permit those of the said religion to make and continue the exercise of the same in all villages and places of our dominion where it was established by them and publicly enjoyed several and divers times in the
25 year 1577. . . .

XXII We ordain that there shall be no difference or distinction made in respect to the said religion, in receiving pupils to be instructed in universities, colleges and schools; nor into receiving the sick and poor into hospitals, retreats and public charities.

J. H. Robinson, *Readings in European History*, vol II, 1906, pp 183 – 5

Questions

*   *a* Why was it necessary to 're-establish' the catholic religion in some places (lines 11 – 12) and how successfully was this done? To which areas of France did this chiefly apply?
    b What is meant by the 'religion called Reformed' (line 18)?
*   *c* What was the significance for the reformed churches of the date 1577?
    d What had been done about 'the fearful disorders and troubles' (line 3) and the 'innumerable factions and sects' (lines 4 – 5), to enable Henry IV to issue this edict?
*   *e* What else did Henry do in his efforts to reassure those of the reformed religion that the edict would and could be enforced?

8   The Huguenot Leadership

The victory could not have been secured without war and the use of the sword. We need not quibble at the fact that Protestant initiative had to pass from those peaceful classes who had allowed themselves to be slaughtered to the only military class that then existed, the nobility. It is a
5 well-known trick of the enemies of liberty to stop at this point, and to appeal to our egalitarian instincts by asking whether one can accept such aristocratic leaders as William the Silent and Coligny. They ought indeed to be accepted, for they inured the people to war, and in consequence the people were in their turn ennobled.
10   Coligny, and his brother, both colonels general of the French Infantry, were the rough, austere instructors of our soldiery of former times. They turned us into a fighting nation of the calibre of the men who, in the aftermath of St Bartholomew when their leaders were slain, could confidently start the war once more in France and the Netherlands, and
15 oblige the Kings to come to terms. These noblemen of the sword, who were the first to form the advance guard of liberty, deserve to be known as men of the people. The historian ought to do for them what was done for a member of the Genoese nobility when, although his class was excluded from office, he performed services for the state. He was
20 rewarded by being degraded from the nobility and advanced to plebian rank. No one deserves this reward more than does Coligny, for it was Coligny who, after a particular treaty, asked the prince de Condé: 'Your treaty protects the nobles, the chateaux and the seigneurs, but who will protect the people of the towns?'

> Jules Michelet, *Histoire de France*, 1855, in J. H. M. Salmon, *The French Wars of Religion*, 1967, p 42

Questions

a   Why does the author think that 'aristocratic leaders' (line 7) should be respected as leaders of the people?
*
b   Why was the prince de Condé generally accepted as the leader of the Huguenots in the early stages of the war?

c   To which treaty might the remark of Coligny, at the end of the extract, refer? What was the importance to the Huguenot cause of 'the people of the towns' (line 24)?
*
d   What were Coligny's greatest services to the Protestant cause? How do his achievements compare with those of Condé?

9   The Catholic League

The municipal and Catholic government of Paris lasted for five years [1588 – 1593] and its history was full of life and emotion. The way was paved for the restoration of Henry IV when this phase in the vast popular drama of the markets and the associations of the artisans had ended. It might be said that the popular movement itself brought about the restoration. Such a movement has served its purpose when popular opinion believes it to have done so, and enlightened opinion desires its conclusion. At the end of 1593, after the conversion of the King of Navarre, the League no longer had any serious purpose in the eyes of the bourgeois, and inevitably it slipped into a decline which led to its ultimate ruin. The entry of Henry IV to Paris was an inevitable fact. The issue was no longer that of Catholicism, but rather that of Spain. The entire vast religious movement that resisted the triumph of the Béarnais had been transformed into an intrigue, and the intrigue collapsed in the face of the general interest of society. . . .

While it was based upon the moral ideals of Catholicism, the League had also to adopt secular doctrines based on the various powers it contained. Submission to princes was in all respects subordinate to submission to the Church. An excommunicated king could not legally govern his subjects. Thence arose the doctrines of regicide and the unbridled demagogy of Leaguer pamphlets. Government no longer assumed the form of monarchy. It mattered little whether the League turned itself into a monarchy or a republic. Its principle was that of Catholicism, and, provided that this was respected, the form of government was merely an accessory issue on which the Church did not trouble itself.

> Jean-Baptiste-Honoré Capefigue, *Histoire de la Réforme, de la Ligue et du règne de Henri IV*, 1834, in J. H. M. Salmon, *The French Wars of Religion*, 1967, pp 55–7

Questions

* *a* Why was the Catholic League originally founded? How had it become so powerful in Paris?
* *b* What effect did preaching 'the doctrines of regicide' (line 20) have on the course of events in the 1580s and 1590s?
* *c* What reason does the author give for the decline of the League?
  d In what sense was the issue, after 1593, 'no longer that of Catholicism, but rather that of Spain' (lines 11–12)?

10 France in 1598

Henri IV's personal prestige and ability were certainly badly needed if the monarchy was to re-establish its position, for the long wars had helped to erode the old bases of royal power. Years of virtual independence had allowed towns and provinces to reinforce or reclaim local rights which limited central intervention, while smaller communities had come more than ever under the equivocal 'protection' of the local nobility. Large numbers of offices had been created and sold during the wars, with serious consequences. . . . The state of the finances was deplorable, and the

disorder of the wars had favoured corruption and speculation on a grand
scale. Local magnates like Damville in Languedoc and the duc d'Épernon
in Angoumois had entrenched their own power at the king's expense.
Awareness of these problems was to combine with the natural in-
clinations of the king and his closest advisers to direct the monarchy into
policies of centralization and deliberate state-building, which would
largely take the form of chipping away at the vast complex of privileges
and liberties which restricted royal power. In certain ways the ex-
periences of the later sixteenth century actually made this task easier; the
League became a kind of bogey in the minds of most men of property,
symbolizing the dangers of extremism, rebellion, and social disorder. . . . The Huguenots and the Leaguers had produced a quantity of
political theorizing in justification of their resistance, calling on every
available argument to diminish the king's personal power; the final effect
was chiefly to discredit a whole range of ideas which would otherwise
have been attractive to defenders of the established order against royal
initiatives. The Estates General, summoned several times during the wars,
had come to appear not only useless but dangerous, and Henri IV took
good care never to fulfil his promises to convene them. The future
belonged to the monarchy, although few of its subjects could have
realised this as the new century began.

Robin Briggs, *Early Modern France 1560–1715*, 1977, pp 33–4

Questions

a   Why should the sale of offices have 'serious consequences (lines 7–8)?
b   What was the League and why had it become a 'bogey' to many
people (line 18)?
*   c   What means did Henri IV use to re-establish the authority of the
crown?
*   d   Besides the political effects discussed here, what other effects did the
wars of religion have on the people of France?
*   e   Do you agree that, in France, 'the future belonged to the monarchy'
(lines 27–8)?

XI The Ottoman Empire

Introduction

The Ottoman empire, in social and governmental structure, was totally different from the rest of Europe. While west European states had developed fixed frontiers and patterns of social organisation, the Turks had an expanding and essentially fluid empire. The continual conquest, which marked the period up to the death of Suleiman the Magnificent, meant that there was an ever-increasing supply of booty to reward the soldiers and of land to provide a more permanent source of income. This was a successful system so long as there were fresh lands to conquer, but the failure of the Turks at Vienna in 1529 marked the beginning of the end of their European conquests.

Communications, too, became a greater problem as the size of the empire increased and it was more and more difficult for the sultan to rule his lands effectively from an army camp somewhere on the frontier, especially as Suleiman's successors were not his equals in ability.

At sea the Ottoman forces were also successful, especially after 1532, when the pirate Barbarossa was appointed admiral of the sultan's fleet. He quickly improved both the actual ships and their use in battle, as the battle of Prevesa in 1538 showed, though this improvement was not maintained.

Socially, Ottoman government was based on slavery. The janissaries, who formed the backbone of the army, were the sons of Christian families taken from them as tribute and brought up as Moslem slaves. Those with ability could reach the top posts in the army and the administration, something which was impossible in other European states. The system had great advantages for the sultan, as he had absolute control over his minister and officials — and whatever money they made from their jobs — and had no need to grant them any privileges; nor had they families expecting rewards and titles.

Further Reading

Fernand Braudel, *The Mediterranean and the Mediterranean World in the Age of Philip II* (Collins, 1972)

Ernle Bradford, *The Great Siege of Malta, 1565* (Penguin, 1964)

1   A System Based on Plunder

For all its external pomp and circumstances, in one important respect the empire of the Ottoman sultans remained — indeed had no alternative but to remain — faithful to the purposes of the tatterdemalion raiding party from which it had evolved; it was organised for plundering and it
5   subsisted on plunder. The resources which sustained the growth of Constantinople into a great metropolis could only be obtained by raiding across the frontiers. Frontier raiding on the massive scale which had now become necessary was work for great armies. Recruitment of these could be — and was — effected in only two ways. Firstly, fiefs could be
10   distributed in return for military service; but . . . land could only be obtained in sufficient quantities by extension of the frontier, that is, by more raiding. Secondly, a slave army could be assembled; but slaves were prizes which could only be won by yet more raiding. The loyalty and enthusiasm of both these military elements depended on the provision of
15   perpetual opportunities for further plunder and upon the presence and obedience of a slave administration; all of which implied more raiding again.

This was a circular system in which everything depended on an inexhaustible supply of slaves, booty and land. Given the comparatively
20   crude and elementary techniques of warfare, transportation, communication and administration available to the Ottoman, which must eventually impose their limitations on the operation of the system, it could not perpetuate itself. Yet disengagement from the pursuit of plunder was unthinkable. . . . The slave soldiery, deprived of the
25   prospect of plunder, would transfer their loyalty from their master, replacing him by a sultan prepared to cater to their appetites and resume the interrupted sequence of conquest and border raiding. The very real possibility of this last development was made abruptly apparent even to a majestic sultan like Suleiman; three years without war produced a serious
30   disturbance among the janissaries of Constantinople in 1525. And in spite of the military triumphs of 1526, events later in the same decade inexorably underlined the other side of the problem, the technical impossibility of conducting spectacularly successful warfare at very long range.

Paul Coles, *The Ottoman Impact on Europe*, 1968, pp 69–70

Questions

a   What were (i) 'fiefs' (line 9) and (ii) 'janissaries' (line 30)?
b   What does the author mean by 'a circular system' (line 18)?
* c   What were the 'military triumphs' (line 31) of 1526? Why did warfare thereafter have to be conducted at 'very long range' (lines 33–4) and why did this cause serious problems for the Ottoman empire?
* d   Why was conquest so easy for the Ottomans until 1526 and what made it more difficult after that date?

2   The Sultan's Admiral

There seems no doubt that it was Doria's successes against the Turkish
navy – and in their own home waters – that prompted Sultan
Suleiman's next action. His Grand Vizier Ibrahim had long been urging
the Sultan to institute closer relations with the new ruler of Algiers. He
5   was eager to cement a friendship between the Sublime Porte and these
Turks in the western Mediterranean who had been enjoying such
overwhelming success against the forces of Spain and the Emperor. In the
spring of 1533 Kheir-ed-Din Barbarossa, Beylerbey of Algiers, received
an ambassador from Constantinople. He was commanded to present
10   himself before Suleiman, Sultan of the Ottomans and 'Allah's Deputy on
Earth', at his earliest convenience. It was a moment of triumph for
Barbarossa. Nearly thirty years previously he had left the Aegean as an
obscure young man in the service of his brother, with two small galleots.
He was now ruler of nearly all Algeria, master of a fleet that terrorised the
15   western Mediterranean, and important enough to have the most
powerful ruler on earth requesting his presence at court. For Barbarossa
must have realised that the Sultan's need for him in Constantinople was
dictated by the fact that he, Barbarossa, had proved himself uniquely
successful against the Christians – especially at sea. . . .
20   The all-important issue was the reorganisation of the fleet: a necessity
which Doria's recent successes had brought home harshly to the Sublime
Porte. It had certainly not escaped the notice of the Grand Vizier that,
whereas Turkish ships under Turkish admirals commanded little success
against the Genoese, Barbarossa and his lieutenants seemed to rule the
25   western Mediterranean as its almost undisputed masters. . . . Barbarossa
was clearly the man to advise on the reorganisation of the navy and,
indeed, even on the design of its ships and equipment.

Ernle Bradford, *The Sultan's Admiral*, 1968, pp 117–19

Questions

a   Who was Doria? What success had he had against the Turkish fleet?
b   What had been Barbarossa's position and status up to this point in his
life?
c   Why did the sultan think that Barbarossa was the right man to reform
the Turkish navy?
   *
d   What success did the Turkish navy have after the reforms and under
Barbarossa's command?
   *
e   What were the main reasons for Turkish success in the Mediterranean
during the first half of the sixteenth century?

3   An Admirer of the System of Government

It is by merit that men rise in the service, a system which ensures that posts
should be assigned only to the competent. . . . Those who receive the

highest offices from the Sultan are for the most part the sons of shepherds
or herdsmen, and so far from being ashamed of their parentage, they
actually glory in it, and consider it a matter for boasting that they owe
nothing to the accident of birth; for they do not believe that high qualities
are either natural or hereditary, nor do they think that they can be handed
down from father to son, but that they are partly the gift of God, and
partly the result of good training, great industry, and unwearied
zeal. . . . Among the Turks, therefore, honours, high posts, and jud-
geships are the rewards of great ability and good service. . . .

This is the reason that they are successful in their undertakings, that
they lord it over others, and are daily extending the bounds of their
empire. These are not our ideas, with us there is no opening left for merit;
birth is the standard for everything; the prestige of birth is the sole key to
advancement in the public service.

> Ogier Ghiselin de Busbecq, Imperial ambassador at Con-
> stantinople, 1555 – 62, in J. B. Ross and M. M. McLaughlin, *The
> Portable Renaissance Reader*, 1977, pp 253 – 4

Questions

a   How was it possible for 'the sons of shepherds or herdsmen' to rise to
*   'the highest offices' (lines 3 – 4)? How high did some of them rise?
b   What kind of 'good training' (line 9) did they receive?
c   Why did the ambassador think that the Turkish system was better
*   than that in his own country?
d   Do you think this system was responsible for the Turkish successes in
the first half of the sixteenth century?

4   An Audience with the Sultan

On our arrival at Amasia we were taken to call on Achmet Pasha (the
chief vizier) and the other pashas – for the Sultan himself was not then in
the town – and commenced our negotiations with them touching the
business entrusted to us by King Ferdinand. The pashas, on their part,
apparently wishing to avoid any semblance of being prejudiced with
regard to these questions, did not offer any strong opposition to the views
we expressed, and told us that the whole matter depended on the Sultan's
pleasure. On his arrival we were admitted to an audience; but the manner
and spirit in which he listened to our address, our arguments, and our
message were by no means favourable.

The Sultan was seated on a very low ottoman, not more than a foot
from the ground, which was covered with a quantity of costly rugs and
cushions of exquisite workmanship; near him lay his bow and arrows.
His air, as I said, was by no means gracious, and his face wore a stern,
though dignified, expression. . . .

After having gone through a pretence of kissing his hand, we were conducted backwards to the wall opposite his seat, care being taken that we should never turn our backs on him. The Sultan then listened to what I had to say; but the language I held was not at all to his taste, for the demands of his Majesty [Ferdinand] breathed a spirit of independence and dignity, which was by no means acceptable to one who deemed that his wish was law; and so he made no answer beyond saying in a tetchy way 'Giusel, giusel', i.e., well, well.

After this we were dismissed to our quarters.

> Ogier Ghiselin de Busbecq, Imperial ambassador at Constantinople, 1555–62, in J. B. Ross and M. M. McLaughlin, *The Portable Renaissance Reader*, 1977, pp 252–3

Questions

* a Who was King Ferdinand? What business might he have had with the sultan?
  b Why were the pashas not in a position to make any decision themselves but 'told us that the whole matter depended on the Sultan's pleasure' (lines 7–8)?
  c Why does the writer think that what he had to say to the sultan 'was by no means acceptable' (line 21)?
* d What agreement did Ferdinand make with the sultan in 1562?

5   The Sultan of the Ottomans

Soleyman's titles resounded through the high council chamber like a roll of drums:

'Sultan of the Ottomans, Allah's deputy on Earth, Lord of the Lords of this World, Possessor of Men's Necks, King of Believers and Unbelievers, King of Kings, Emperor of the East and West, Emperor of the Chakans of Great Authority, Prince and Lord of the most happy Constellation, Majestic Caesar, Seal of Victory, Refuge of all the People in the whole World, the Shadow of the Almighty dispensing Quiet in the Earth.'

His ministers, admirals, and generals prostrated themselves and withdrew. It was the year 1564, and Soleyman the First, Sultan of Turkey, was seventy years old. He had just taken the decision to attack the island of Malta in the spring of the following year.

His had been a life of unparalleled distinction from the moment when he had succeeded his father, Selim, at the age of twenty-six. Known in his own country as the Lawgiver, and throughout Europe as Soleyman the Magnificent, he had truly earned these appellations. He had reformed and improved the government and administration of Turkey, and had made her the greatest military state in the world. He was unequalled as a statesman, and was a poet in his own right.

If the Turkish people for these reasons called him 'The Lawgiver', the

people of Europe for their part had good reasons for conceding to him the respectful title of 'The Magnificent'. His conquests alone justified it, and Europeans have always lavished more respect upon conquerors than upon
25 lawgivers. In the course of his Sultanate, Soleyman had added to his dominions, Aden, Algiers, Baghdad, Belgrade, Budapest, Nakshivan, Rhodes, Rivan, Tabriz and Temesvar. Under him the Ottoman Empire had attained the peak of its glory. His galleys swept the seas from the Atlantic to the Indian Ocean, and his kingdom stretched from Austria to
30 the Persian Gulf, and the shores of the Arabian Sea. Only at the walls of Vienna in 1529 had his armies faltered.

Ernle Bradford, *The Great Siege: Malta 1565*, 1964, pp 13-14

Questions

a Why did Suleiman decide to attack Malta? What was the outcome of the attack?
* *b* What had made it possible for Suleiman to achieve so many conquests?
* *c* Why had the Turks failed to take Vienna?
* *d* Do you agree that Suleiman deserved the title of 'The Magnificent'?

6 The Beginning of Ottoman Decline

1566 was a turning point in the institution of the Sultan. It was almost as if history had deliberately arranged that the first ten Sultans (with one exception) should have been the best of all the Empire's rulers and the next thirteen (with two exceptions) the worst. . . .
5   The Ottoman Empire was particularly vulnerable to incompetent leadership because it was based upon a more complete form of despotism than any other regime in Europe. The Sultan was the head of the Religious Institution and the Ruling Institution. . . . The power of the Sultan can be gauged from the fact that all members of the Ruling
10 Institution, the Grand Vizier included, were virtually slaves and could be dealt with summarily on the Sultan's orders. . . .
    To the outside world the most obvious manifestation of Ottoman decline was military. In 1566 the Turks controlled the entire eastern Mediterranean area, ruled most of Hungary, and had a long-standing
15 military and diplomatic connection with . . . France. In 1699 the Turks were forced to sign the humiliating Treaty of Carlowitz, acknowledging the loss of most of Hungary. . . .
    The military reverses suffered by the Ottomans were due partly to the growth of more competent and professional armies in Europe . . . and
20 partly to the internal crises of the Empire itself. The tendency of the janissaries to involve themselves in politics removed the advantage which they had once possessed as specialized infantry. . . .
    Political crises and military disasters coincided with economic pro-

blems as the régime faced the prospect of rapidly diminishing
25   resources. . . .

The expansion of the Empire's frontiers had meant that each campaign
had to be fought over larger distances and thus became progressively
more expensive. Military success meant that much of the cost could be
recovered from the newly conquered areas. . . . When the victories
30   turned to defeat the [war] machine could no longer sustain itself and had
to be financed by other means. . . .

Meanwhile, the position of the Ottoman Empire in the world trading
network had altered substantially. . . . The importance of Ottoman
control over the overland routes to the East therefore declined rapidly
35   towards the end of the century, and the decreased volume of commerce
caused an irreplaceable loss of revenue.

Stephen J. Lee, *Aspects of European History 1494–1789*, 1978, pp
80–86

Questions

a   What was the effect on the empire's system of government of a
*   succession of weak sultans?
b   What were the advantages and disadvantages for France of the links
with the Turks?
c   Why did the Turkish army become weaker after 1566?
d   Why did the 'overland routes to the East' (line 34) and the associated trade become so much less important during the sixteenth century?
*   e   Do you think a strong sultan could have prevented the decline of the
Ottoman empire?
*   f   What events proved to the Europeans that the Turks were no longer
as powerful as they had been? Were the Europeans able to take
advantage of this?

7   Was Lepanto a Turning-Point?

The Ottoman naval defeat in 1571 had impelled the Muslim empire to
recover its naval power and to continue its advance into the western
portions of the Islamic world. From either the Christian or the Muslim
point of view, important imperial campaigns with far-reaching con-
5   sequences for Mediterranean and European states took place after the
galley battle of 1571. At the level of diplomatic history, the turning point
in the post-Lepanto imperial struggles was the battle of Alcazar, which
was fought in Morocco during the summer of 1578. Linked to the history
of Ottoman–Spanish warfare and diplomacy, this new information
10   shifts the locus of the Christian–Muslim disengagement in 1580 from the
eastern and central Mediterranean to Morocco where the subsequent
diplomatic manoeuvres of Ahmad al-Mansūr led to the skilful creation of

a Muslim buffer state. The battle of Lepanto, therefore, did not directly
set the conditions for the neutralization of the Mediterranean but instead
encouraged further warfare until the question of who controlled North
Africa was settled in favour of the Ottomans. . . .

If the battle of Lepanto is not the climactic event it appeared to be, how
does this last grand galley battle fit into the history of the
Mediterranean? . . . It could be argued that the Turks won the
Mediterranean wars, having, after the battle of Alcazar in 1578, forced
the Christian states back into the European land mass. . . . Integrating
the records of two Mediterranean civilizations, the battle of Lepanto takes
its place in Mediterranean history as a major frontier clash in the brutal
struggle between two different and relatively powerful civilizations.

Andrew C. Hess, *The Battle of Lepanto and its Place in Mediterranean History*, Past and Present, no. 57, 1972, pp 70–72

Questions

a   Who fought the battle of Lepanto and why is it generally regarded as
so important?
b   What is meant by calling this battle 'a major frontier clash' (line 23)?
c   Who fought the battle of Alcazar and with what result? Why was it
important for (i) Spain and Portugal and (ii) the Ottoman empire?
*
d   In what sense did Morocco subsequently become 'a Muslim buffer
state' (line 13)?
*
e   Why did both the Ottoman empire and Spain accept the 'neutralization' (line 14) of the Mediterranean after 1580?

8   The Sultan Agrees to a Truce with Spain

Your ambassador who is currently at our imperial court submitted a
petition to our throne of dignity and royal home of justice. Our exalted
threshold of the centre of greatness, our imperial court of omnipotent
power is indeed the sanctuary of commanding sultans and the stronghold
of the rulers of the age.

A petition of friendship and devotion came from your side. For the
safety and security of state and the affluence and tranquillity of your
subjects, you wished friendship with our home of majestic greatness. In
order to arrange a structure for peace and to set up conditions for a treaty,
our justice-laden imperial agreement was issued on these matters. Also,
regarding whatever was written and described in detail, our noble
knowledge and world-inclusive sovereignty comprehended and included all of it. . . .

Since our most pious of sultans is to be the [friend of] your friends and
the enemy of your enemies, your hope which existed in this matter
received our imperial acceptance. . . .

It is necessary . . . when it arrives . . . that your irregulars and corsairs

who are producing ugliness and wickedness on land and sea do not harm
the subjects of our protected territories and that they be stopped and
20 controlled.

On the point of faithfulness and integrity let you be staunch and
constant and let you respect the condition of the truce. From this side also
no situation will come into existence at all contrary to the truce. Whether
it be our naval commanders on the sea, our volunteer captains [corsairs]
25 or our commanders who are on the frontiers of the protected territories,
our world-obeyed orders will be sent and damage and difficulties will not
reach your country or states and the businessmen who come from that
area from any one.

In our imperial time and at our royal abode of happiness it is indeed
30 decided that the prosperity of times comes into being. In the same
manner, if the building of peace and prosperity and the construction of a
treaty and of security, are your aims, without delay send your man to our
fortunate throne and make known your position.

Letter from the court of Sultan Murad III to Philip II of Spain,
August 1580, in A. C. Hess, *The Battle of Lepanto and its Place in
Mediterranean History*, Past and Present, no. 57, 1972, pp. 68–9

Questions

a   Stripped of all the elaborate wording, what is the sultan actually
agreeing to do?

b   Who are meant by 'your irregulars and corsairs' (line 17)? How
far was it possible for them to be controlled by their nominal rulers?

*   c   Why should Spanish 'businessmen' (line 27) wish to visit the
Ottoman empire?

*   d   Why did a truce at this time suit both the sultan and the king of Spain?

*   e   What was settled by the truce and how long did it last?

9   The Ottoman Empire

Selim died shortly after his victories, in 1520, on the road to Adrianople.
His son Sulaimān succeeded him unchallenged. To Sulaimān was to fall
the honour of consolidating the might of the Ottoman Empire. . . . He
arrived at an opportune moment, it is true. In 1521, he seized Belgrade,
5 the gateway to Hungary; in July, 1522, he laid siege to Rhodes, which fell
in December of the same year: once the formidable and influential fortress
of the Knights of St John had fallen, the entire eastern Mediterranean lay
open to his youthful ambition. There was now no reason why the master
of so many Mediterranean shores should not build a fleet. His subjects and
10 the Greeks, including those who inhabited Venetian islands, were to
provide him with the indispensable manpower. Would the reign of
Sulaimān, ushered in by these brilliant victories, have been so illustrious
had it not been for his father's conquest of Egypt and Syria?

The reign of Sulaiman was at the same time an age of victorious warfare, of widespread construction and of substantial legislative activity. Sulaimān bore the title of Kanūnī, or law-maker, indicative of a revival of law studies and the existence of a special class of jurists in the states under his rule and above all at Constantinople. His legal code so successfully regulated the judicial machinery that it was said that Henry VIII of England sent a legal mission to Constantinople to study its workings. . . .

The more one thinks about it, the more convinced one becomes of the striking similarities, between East and West, worlds very different it is true, but not always divergent. Experts in Roman law and learned interpreters of the Koran formed a single vast army, working in the East as in the West to enhance the prerogative of princes. It would be both rash and inaccurate to attribute the progress made by monarchy entirely to the zeal, calculations and devotions of these men. All monarchies remained charismatic. And there was always the economy. Nevertheless, this army of lawyers, whether eminent or modest, was fighting on the side of the large state. It detested and strove to destroy all that stood in the way of state expansion. . . . Turkey, now becoming partly against her own will a modern state, appointed to the conquered eastern provinces of Asia, increasing numbers of half-pay farmers, who lived off the revenues they collected but transmitted the bulk'of it to Istanbul; she also appointed increasing numbers of paid civil servants who, in exchange for specific service, preferably in the towns easiest to administer, would receive a salary from the imperial treasury. More and more of these officials tended to be renegade Christians, who thus gradually infiltrated the ruling class of the Ottoman Empire. They were recruited through the *devshirme*, a sort of 'tribute which consisted of taking away from their homes in the Balkans a certain number of Christian children, usually under the age of five.' . . .

Venality, detrimental to the state, was likewise embedded in Turkish institutions. . . . The need to *corteggiare* one's superiors, to offer them substantial gifts, obliged every state servant to reimburse himself regularly, at the expense of his inferiors and of the localities he administered, and so on down the scale. The organised misappropriation of public funds operated throughout the hierarchy. The Ottoman Empire was the victim of these insatiable officer-holders, obliged by the very tyranny of usage to be insatiable. The individual who drew most benefit from this daylight robbery was the grand vizier. . . .

In the Turkish Empire however, the enormous fortune of a vizier was always at the disposal of the sultan, who could seize it upon the death, whether natural or otherwise, of his minister. In this way, the Turkish state participated in the habitual peculation of its officers.

Fernand Braudel, *The Mediterranean and the Mediterranean World in the Age of Philip II*, trans. S. Reynolds, vol II, 1972, pp 668–9, 683–5, 689–90

Questions

a What was the significance for the future of the Turkish conquest of Egypt, Syria and Rhodes?

b In what ways could 'this army of lawyers' (lines 29–30) 'enhance the prerogative of princes' (line 26)?

* c Why was an increasing number of officials needed in the Ottoman empire?

* d Why was venality 'detrimental to the state' (line 44) and who suffered most because of it?

* e How would you describe the position of the 'grand vizier' (line 52) and what kind of man usually held this office?

f From the extract, what were the most important achievements of Suleiman?